Globa

The Battle Against the World Trade Organization and Corporate Rule

Edited by Kevin Danaher and Roger Burbach

Common Courage Press
Monroe, Maine

Cover design by Matt Wuerker

Library of Congress Cataloging-In-Publication Data is available from the publisher.

Common Courage Press
Box 702
Monroe, Maine 04951
Phone: (207) 525-0900
FAX: (207) 525-3068
www.commoncouragepress.com
email: orders-info@commoncouragepress.com

First Printing

Contents

Acknowledgments

We would like to thank all the organizations who so kindly allowed us to use their material in this book: *La Jornada* (Chapter 3), Third World Network (Chapter 5), FAIR, the Media Watch Group (Chapter 7), Focus on the Global South (Chapters 14 & 20), *Rachel's Environment & Health Weekly* (Chapter 17), *The Nation* (Chapter 19), *The New Internationalist* (Chapters 20, 22, 23).

Special thanks Matt Wuerker for his design skills, and to Arthur Stamoulis, Greg Bates and all the other great folks at Common Courage Press who pulled out all the stops in order to get this book produced in record time.

And most of all, thanks to the tens of thousands of people who turned out on the streets of Seattle to send a clear message to the rulers of the planet that we are determined to have a new global system, whether the rulers like it or not!

Introduction:
People Making History

November 30, 1999 marked a turning point in history. Tens of thousands of ordinary citizens took to the streets of Seattle to stop the World Trade Organization (WTO) from conducting 'business as usual' (i.e., making rules for the entire planet that mainly serve the interests of large corporations).

Seattle marked a turning point in a number of ways. Never before had so much anti-corporate critique appeared in the corporate-controlled media. The *Los Angeles Times* opined: "On the tear gas shrouded streets of Seattle, the unruly forces of democracy collided with the elite world of trade policy. And when the meeting ended in failure on Friday the elitists had lost and the debate had changed forever."

This penetration of the corporate media with an anti-corporate message built on a growing public distrust of the corporate "free trade" agenda. A late-1999 poll by the University of Maryland found that 78 percent of Americans thought the WTO should pay more attention to environmental and labor concerns. A *Business Week* poll conducted during the protests found that 52 percent of Americans sympathized with the protestors.

Seattle marked the greatest failure of elite trade diplomacy since the end of World War II. Even in 1982, when the Reagan administration tried—and failed—to force through a new round of negotiations for trade liberalization, there was at least a declaration and future work agenda issued at the end of the conference. Not so in Seattle. The Clinton team, led by U.S. Trade Representative Charlene Barshefsky, handled the controversy in Seattle so ineptly that the talks ended in total collapse.

This was a huge blow to the Clinton administration, which had based most of its foreign policy on pushing for more international privileges for corporations. As the *New York Times* reported on February 19, 2000, "Administration officials now concede that [the Seattle] meeting was among the biggest blunders of Mr. Clinton's second term."

Most importantly, Seattle was the coming out party for a new global movement for citizen power that will certainly go on to bigger and better things. A remarkable diversity of interests came together with a unified critique of corporate rule. Trade unionists, environmentalists, human rights activists, church groups, AIDS activists, family farmers, and grassroots organizers from around the world all united against the WTO because it promotes the interests of large corporations over the interests of people and nature.

There were actually two battles in Seattle. The unity of the opposition movement in the streets exacerbated the disunity among the elites inside the WTO conference. Because the groups opposing the WTO included traditional Democratic Party constituencies (especially organized labor), President Clinton tried to calm their anger by giving a speech calling for international standards to defend the rights of workers. This emphasis on labor rights scared elitist third world leaders whose main bargaining chip with the transnational corporations is to offer up their working classes at low wages.

Plus, Clinton's speech came on top of a U.S. tradition of dominating international trade talks and bullying other countries, so third world leaders were in no mood to be lectured by a U.S. president. Even European governments were reluctant to go along with U.S. insistence on lowering agricultural trade barriers and allowing the unrestricted flow of genetically modified foods. So, with the protestors outside disrupting Clinton's plan for a free trade love-fest, the delegates inside fell to squabbling among themselves and the talks collapsed.

The people's victory in Seattle has been like a huge shot of adrenaline for the global democracy movement. Planning meetings that formerly drew ten people now draw fifty. Demonstrations that previously took months to organize now come together in weeks. Almost before the tear gas had cleared in Seattle, the movement was abuzz with plans for massive demonstrations April 16–17 at the Washington, DC spring meetings of the World Bank and International Monetary Fund.

The First Global Revolution

We can now envision the formation of a truly global movement capable of challenging the most powerful institutions on the planet. As you will see in the concluding section of this book, progressive organizations are drawing up plans for how we could run the global economy in a life-centered way rather than a money-centered way. The money paradigm that has ruled for so long is now losing public support. And the life paradigm, which emphasizes human rights and saving the environment, is gaining support. Transnational unity at the grassroots level is strengthening, while transnational unity at the elite level is fraying.

If we look closely we can see the pieces of the first global revolution being put together. Every revolution up until now has been a national revolution, aimed at seizing control of a national government. But the blatant corporate bias of global rule-making institutions such as the IMF, World Bank and WTO have forced the grassroots democracy movement to start planning a global revolution. It is a revolution in values as well as institutions. It seeks to replace the money values of the current system with the life values of a truly democratic system.

Just look at the various components of this global revolution, all of which are growing vigorously:

• The world's trade union movement is undergoing a double transformation. More and more unionists are realizing that organizing within a national context is no longer adequate for dealing with globe-spanning corporations, so unions must increase the amount and sophistication of cross-border solidarity. Trade unions are also expanding their traditionally narrow shop-floor approach, and are replacing it with what is often called social unionism or community-based unionism, which seeks out alliances with churches, NGOs, and other organizations in civil society. The victory in Seattle gave this trend a significant boost.

• The corporate accountability movement has developed great skill at pressuring corporations to change their objectionable policies, and now the movement is moving up to the next level: questioning the very right of these corporations to exist. People are learning that corporations exist because we, the sovereign citizens, charter them and give them a piece of our sovereignty. What can be given can be taken away, if enough citizens demand it. People are talking about organizing a campaign to pass an amendment to the U.S. Constitution that says: "A corporation is not a human being."

• There is a diverse range of organizations working for a return-to-the-local in terms of citizen empowerment. These efforts span the political spectrum from left to right, yet they agree that as much decision-making as possible (political and economic) should take place at the local level, where people actually live. This is in sharp contrast to the agenda pushed by the likes of the WTO, IMF and World Bank.

• The traditional separation between environmental struggles and social justice struggles is being bridged by more and more groups. Activists are going beyond "end-of-pipeline" politics, whereby we react to the policies of elites by trying to soften their impact on people and nature. Instead we are saying let's go inside and change the machinery that is producing bad policy in the first place. It's like the difference between jumping in a river to save each drowning child, and going up-river to stop whoever is throwing the kids in the water in the first place.

What these various movements have in common is the goal of expanding the practice of democracy to include the economic realm. They harken back to the origins of the word democracy in the Greek roots 'demos' meaning people, and 'kratos' meaning rule. It took hundreds of years to achieve the separation of church and state, and now we are in the middle of a long struggle to achieve the separation of corporations and the state.

There *will* some day be a democratic global economy. The question is: will that take us 500 years or 50 years or 15 years to achieve?

This book is designed to be a tool in the struggle to democratize the global economy. It provides an analysis of what actually happened in Seattle, in stark contrast to the partial and distorted version presented in the corporate media. We also address many of the questions that now confront the movement: how do we bridge divisions of race, class, gender and nationality; how can we develop alternative institutions that can make rules for the global economy *democratically*; and how can we replace the dominance of money values with a system that venerates life in all its forms.

We conclude the book with resources and ways you can get involved in this historic movement. In the past, we book producers had a problem collecting enough resources to fill a "What To Do" section of a book like this. Now the problem is a better one: there are so many organizations working on these issues that we could fill an entire book with just organizational references. We have tried to provide references to key groups working on what we believe to be cutting edge issues in the struggle to democratize the global economy. We apologize to those of you we left out.

No social advance rolls in on the wheels of inevitability. It comes through the tireless efforts and persistent work of dedicated individuals.

Rev. Martin Luther King, Jr.

Section One

What Happened In Seattle and What Does It Mean?

There were so many different organizations and interests represented in the Seattle WTO protests that it would take many volumes to represent them all fairly. We have included here articles that give a taste of the complexity of the event from a range of perspectives.

Paul Hawken, in "Skeleton Woman Comes to Seattle," artfully weaves together the street scenes and the policy debates.

In "How We Really Shut Down the WTO," Starhawk gives her unique perspective on the art and science of organizing mass, nonviolent civil disobedience utilizing a democratic, affinity group model.

The "Revolt of the Globalized," by Luis Hernandez Navarro, is a Mexican journalist's view of the protest's historical significance and how it fits in with other movements around the world.

Ken Butigan, in "We Traveled to Seattle: A Pilgrimage of Transformation," locates the protest within a noble tradition of mass mobilizing as pioneered by Gandhi and Martin Luther King, Jr.

In "Revolt of the Developing Nations," Martin Khor emphasizes the splits between developing country leaders and their counterparts in the industrialized countries as factors in the demise of the WTO talks.

Susan George makes a strong case for either "Fixing or Nixing the WTO" by showing how strong and sophisticated the opposition has become in recent years.

In his devastating critique of the corporate media ("Prattle in Seattle: How the Media Misrepresented the Protest"), Seth Ackerman provides chapter and verse of how most of the commercial media just plain got it wrong.

Medea Benjamin concludes the section with "The Debate Over Tactics," focusing on the question of 'violence' and the process by which we should decide on the appropriate tactics for building a mass movement.

The highly successful demonstration of "people's power" at the World Trade Organization provides impressive testimony to the effectiveness of educational and organizing efforts designed for the long term, carried out with dedication and persistence, based on open and honest interchange, and guided by careful evaluation of attainable goals and future prospects. That is the way to build authentic popular movements, worldwide in scope, varied in constituencies, linked in solidarity and sympathetic concern. Many obstacles stand in the way towards a world in which people control their lives, their work, their social interactions in every domain. Coercive and illegitimate institutions will not easily relinquish their power. Internal conflict is inevitable, and welcome; no one has a magic claim to truth and understanding. Also inevitable, and far from welcome, will be the attempts of elitist elements to exploit, undermine, and seek to take over popular movements that are created by the hard work of truly committed participants. The needs are great, the prospects inspiring. What has taken place in Seattle offers real opportunities for a long step forward in the everlasting struggle to expand the realms of freedom and justice.

Noam Chomsky

1

Skeleton Woman Visits Seattle

Paul Hawken

When I was able to open my eyes, I saw lying next to me a young man, 19, maybe 20 at the oldest. He was in shock, twitching and shaking uncontrollably from being tear-gassed and pepper-sprayed at close range. His burned eyes were tightly closed, and he was panting irregularly. Then he passed out. He went from excruciating pain to unconsciousness on a sidewalk wet from the water that a medic had poured over him to flush his eyes.

More than 700 organizations and between 40,000 and 60,000 people took part in the protests against the World Trade Organization's Third Ministerial, November 30-December 3, 1999. These groups and citizens sense a cascading loss of human and labor rights in the world. Seattle was not the beginning but simply the most striking expression of citizens struggling against a worldwide corporate-financed oligarchy: in effect, a plutocracy.

Oligarchy and plutocracy are not polite terms. They often are used to describe 'other' countries where a small group of wealthy people rule, but not the "first world": the United States, Japan, Germany or Canada. The WTO, however, is trying to solidify that corporate plutocracy. Already, the world's top 200 companies have twice the assets of the poorest 80 percent of the world's people. Global corporations represent a new empire whether they admit it or not. With massive amounts of capital at their disposal, which can be used to influence politicians and the public, they threaten and diminish all democratic institutions. Corporate free market policies subvert culture and community, a true tyranny. The American Revolution occurred because of crown-chartered corporate abuse, a "remote tyranny" in Thomas Jefferson's words. To see Seattle as a singular event, as did most of the media, is like viewing the battles of Lexington and Concord as meaningless skirmishes.

But the mainstream media—consistently problematic in their coverage of any type of protest—had an even more difficult time understanding and covering both the issues and activists in Seattle. No charismatic leader led. No religious figure engaged in direct action. No movie stars starred. There was no alpha group. The Ruckus Society, Rainforest Action Network, Global Exchange, Art and Revolution and hundreds more were there, coordinated primarily by cell phones, email, and the Direct Action Network. They were up against the Seattle Police Department, the Secret Service, and the FBI, to say nothing of the media coverage and the WTO itself.

Contrary to the negative portrayal in the corporate media, the protestors were organized, educated and determined. They were human rights activists, labor activists, indigenous people, people of faith, steel workers, and farmers. They were forest activists, environmentalists, social justice workers, students and teachers. And they wanted the World Trade Organization to listen. They were speaking on behalf of a world that has not been made better by globalization. Income disparity is growing rapidly. The difference between the top and bottom 20 percent has doubled in the past 30 years. The richest 20 percent of the world's people consume 86 percent of the world's resources, while he poorest 20 percent get just one percent.

The apologists for globalization cannot support their contention that open borders, reduced tariffs and forced trade benefit the poorest three billion people in the world. Globalization does, however, create the concentrations of capital seen in northern financial and industrial centers, such as Seattle itself. Since the people promoting globalized free trade policies live in those cities, it is natural that they should be biased.

The demonstrators and activists who showed up in Seattle were not against trade. They do demand proof that shows when and how trade benefits workers and the environment here and abroad. Since that proof has yet to be offered, the protestors came to Seattle to hold the WTO accountable.

On the morning of November 30th, I walked toward the Convention Center with Randy Hayes, the founder of Rainforest Action Network. As soon as we turned the corner on First Street and Pike Avenue, we could hear drums, chants, sirens, roars. At Fifth, police stopped us. We could go no farther without credentials. Ahead of us were thousands of protesters. Beyond them was a large cordon of gas-masked and riot-shielded police, an armored personnel carrier, and fire trucks. On one corner was Niketown. On the other, the Sheraton Hotel, through which there was a passage to the Convention Center. The cordon of police in front of us tried to prevent more protestors from joining those who blocked the entrances to the Convention Center. Randy was a credentialed WTO delegate, which means he could join the proceedings as an observer. He showed his pass to the officer, who thought it looked like me. The officer joked with us, kidded Randy about having my credential and then winked and let us both through.

The police were still relaxed at that point. Ahead of us crowds were milling and moving. The "anarchists" were there, maybe 40 in all, dressed in black pants, black bandanas, black balaclavas, and jackboots, one of two groups identifiable by costume. The other was a group of 300 children who had dressed brightly as turtles in the Sierra Club march the day before. The costumes were part of a serious complaint against the WTO. When the United States attempted to block imports of shrimp caught in the same nets that capture and drown 150,000 sea turtles each year, the WTO called the block "arbitrary and unjustified." Thus far, in every environmental dispute that has come before the WTO, its three-judge panels—which deliberate in secret—have ruled for business, against the environment. The panel members are selected from lawyers and officials who are not educated in biology, the environment, social issues or anthropology.

Opening ceremonies for the World Trade Organization's Third Ministerial were to have been held that Tuesday morning at the Paramount Theater near the Convention Center. Police had ringed the theater with Metro buses touching bumper to bumper. The protesters surrounded the outside of that steel circle. Only a few hundred of the 5,000 delegates made it inside, as police were unable to provide safe corridors for members and ambassadors. The theater was virtually empty when U.S. trade representative and meeting co-chair Charlene Barshefsky was to have delivered the opening keynote. Instead, she was captive in her hotel a block from the meeting site. WTO Executive Director Michael Moore was said to have been apoplectic. Mayor Paul Schell stood despondently near the stage.

Since no scheduled speakers were present, Kevin Danaher, Medea Benjamin, and Juliette Beck from Global Exchange went to the lectern and offered to begin a dialogue in the meantime. The WTO had not been able to come to a pre-meeting consensus on the draft agenda. The NGO community, however, had drafted a consensus agreement about globalization, and the three thought this would be a good time to present it, even if the hall had only a desultory number of delegates. Although the three were credentialed observers to the conference, the sound system was quickly turned off and the police arm-locked and handcuffed them. Medea's wrist was sprained. All were dragged off stage and expelled from the hall.

The expulsions mirrored how the WTO has operated since its birth in 1995. Listening to people is not its strong point. WTO rules run roughshod over local laws and regulations. The WTO agenda relentlessly pursues the elimination of any strictures on the free flow of trade, including how a product is made, by whom it is made, and what happens when it is made. By doing so, the WTO is eliminating the ability of countries and regions to set standards, to express values, or to determine what they do or don't support. Child labor, prison labor, forced labor, and substandard wages and working conditions cannot be used as a basis to discriminate against goods. Nor can environmental destruction, habitat loss, toxic waste production, and the presence of transgenic materials or synthetic hormones be used as the basis to screen or stop goods from entering a country. Under WTO rules, the boycott of South Africa would not have existed. If the world could vote on the WTO, would it pass? Not one country of the 135 member states of the WTO has held a plebiscite to see if their people support the WTO mandate. The people trying to meet in the Green Rooms at the Seattle Convention Center were not elected. Even Michael Moore was not elected.

But while the Global Exchange disruptors were temporarily silenced, the main organizer of the downtown protests, the Direct Action Network, was executing a plan that was working brilliantly outside the Convention Center. The plan was simple: insert groups of trained non-violent activists into key points downtown, making it impossible for delegates to move. DAN had hoped that 1,500 people would show up. Close to 10,000 did. The 2,000 people who began the march to the Convention Center at 7 a.m. from Victor Steinbrueck Park and Seattle Central Community College were composed of affinity groups and clusters whose responsibility was to block key intersections and entrances. Participants had trained for many weeks in some cases, for many hours in others. Each affinity group had its own mission and was self-organized.

Protestors had divided the streets around the Convention Center into 13 sections and individual groups and clusters were responsible for holding these sections. There were also "flying groups" that moved at will from section to section, backing up groups under attack as needed. The groups were further divided into those willing to be arrested, and those who were not. As a group of protestors was beaten, gassed, clubbed, and pushed back, a new group would replace them.

Throughout most of the day, using a variety of techniques, groups held intersections and key areas downtown. The protests were organized through a network of cell phones, bullhorns, and signals. All decisions prior to the demonstrations were reached by consensus. Minority views here heeded and included. The basic rules shared by all were: no violence, physical or verbal, no weapons, no drugs or alcohol. There were no charismatic leaders barking orders. There was no command chain. There was no one in charge: many lieutenants, no generals. Police said that they were not prepared for the level of violence, but, as one protestor later commented, what they were unprepared for was a network of non-violent protestors totally committed to one goal: shutting down the WTO.

Meanwhile, Moore and Barshefsky's frustration was growing by the minute. Their anger and disappointment was shared by Madeleine Albright, the Clinton advance team, and, back in Washington, by chief of staff John Podesta. This was to have been a celebration, a victory, one of the crowning achievements to showcase the Clinton administration, the moment when it would consolidate its free trade policies, allowing the Democrats to show multinational corporations that they could deliver the goods. This was to have been Barshefsky's moment, an event that would give her the inside track to become Secretary of Commerce in the Gore Administration. This was to have been Michael Moore's moment, reviving what had been a mediocre political ascendancy in New Zealand.

If the as-yet unapproved draft agenda were ever ratified, the Europeans could no longer block or demand labeling on genetically modified crops without being slapped with punitive lawsuits and tariffs. The draft also contains provisions that would allow all water in the world to be privatized. It would allow corporations patent protection on all forms of life, even genetic material in cultural use for thousands of years. Farmers who have spent thousands of years growing crops in a valley in India could, within a decade, be required to pay for their water. They could also find that they would have to purchase seeds containing genetic traits their ancestors developed, from companies that have engineered the seeds not to reproduce unless the farmer annually buys expensive chemicals to restore seed viability. If this happens, the CEOs of Novartis and Enron, two of the companies creating the seeds and privatizing the water, will have more money. What will Indian farmers have?

But the perfect moment for Barshefsky, Moore and Monsanto didn't arrive. The meeting couldn't start. Demonstrators were everywhere. Private security guards locked down the hotels. The downtown stores were shut. Hundreds of delegates were on the street trying to get into the Convention Center. No one could help them. For WTO delegates accustomed to an ordered corporate or governmental world, it was a calamity.

Up Pike toward Seventh and to Randy's and my right on Sixth, protestors faced armored cars, horses, and police in full riot gear. In between, demonstrators ringed the Sheraton to prevent an alternative entry to the Convention Center. At one point, police guarding the steps to the lobby pummeled and broke through a crowd of protestors to let eight delegates in. On Sixth Street, Sergeant Richard Goldstein asked demonstrators seated on the street in front of the police line "to cooperate" and move back 40 feet. No one understood why, but that hardly mattered. No one was going to move. He announced that "chemical irritants" would be used if they did not leave. The police were anonymous. No facial expressions, no face. You could not see their eyes. They were masked Hollywood caricatures burdened with 60 to 70 pounds of weaponry. These were not the men and women of the 6th precinct. They were the Gang Squads and the SWAT teams of the Tactical Operations Divisions, closer in training to soldiers from the School of the Americas than local cops on the beat. Behind them and around were special forces from the FBI, the Secret Service, even the CIA.

The police were almost motionless. They were equipped with U.S. military standard M40A1 double canister gas masks; uncalibrated, semi-automatic, high velocity Autocockers loaded with solid plastic shot; Monadnock disposable plastic cuffs, Nomex slash-resistant gloves, Commando boots, Centurion tactical leg guards, combat harnesses, DK5-H pivot-and-lock riot face shields, black Monadnock P24 polycarbonate riot batons with TrumBull stop side handles, No. 2 continuous discharge CS (ortochlorobenzylidene-malononitrile) chemical grenades, M651 CN (chloroacetophenone) pyrotechnic grenades, T16 Flameless OC Expulsion Grenades, DTCA rubber bullet grenades (Stingers), M-203 (40mm) grenade launchers, First Defense MK-46 Oleo-resin Capsicum (OC) aerosol tanks with hose and wands, .60 cali-ber rubber ball impact munitions, lightweight tactical Kevlar com-posite ballistic helmets, combat butt packs, 30 caliber thirty-round mag pouches, and Kevlar body armor. The police did not have visible badges or forms of identification.

The demonstrators seated in front were equipped with hooded jackets for protection against rain and chemicals. They carried toothpaste and baking powder for protection of their skin, and wet cotton cloths impregnated with vinegar to cover their mouths and noses after a tear-gas release. In their backpacks were bottled water and food for the day ahead.

Ten Koreans came around the corner carrying a 10-foot ban-ner protesting genetically modified foods. They were impeccable in white robes, sashes, and headbands. One was a priest. They played flutes and drums and marched straight toward the police and behind the seated demonstrators. Everyone cheered at the sight and chanted "The whole world is watching." The sun broke through the gauzy clouds. It was a beautiful day. Over cell phones, we could hear the cheers coming from the labor rally at the foot-ball stadium. The air was still and quiet.

At 10 a.m. the police fired the first seven canisters of tear gas into the crowd. The whitish clouds wafted slowly down the street. The seated protestors were overwhelmed, yet most did not budge. Police poured over them. Then came the truncheons, and the rub-ber bullets. I was with a couple hundred people who had ringed the hotel, arms locked. We watched as long as we could until the tear gas slowly enveloped us. We were several hundred feet from Sgt. Goldstein's 40-foot "cooperation" zone. Police pushed and truncheoned their way through and behind us. We had covered our faces with rags and cloth, snatching glimpses of the people being clubbed in the street before shutting our eyes. The gas was a fog through which people moved in slow, strange dances of shock and pain and resistance.

Tear gas is a misnomer. Think about feeling asphyxiated and blinded. Breathing becomes labored. Vision is blurred. The mind is disoriented. The nose and throat burn. It's not a gas, it's a drug. Gas-masked police hit, pushed, and speared us with the ends of their batons. We all sat down, hunched over, and locked arms more tightly. By then, the tear gas was so strong our eyes couldn't open. One by one, our heads were jerked back from the rear, and pepper was sprayed directly into each eye. It was very professional. Like hair spray from a stylist. Sssst. Sssst.

Pepper spray is derived from cayenne peppers. It is food-grade, pure enough to be used in salsa. The spray used in Seattle is the strongest available, containing 10 percent to 15 percent Oleoresin Capsicum, with a 1.5 to 2.0 million Scoville heat unit rating. One to three Scoville units are when your tongue can first detect hotness. (The jalapeño pepper is rated between 2,500 to 5,000 Scoville units. The habanero, usually considered the hottest pepper in the world, is rated around 300,000 Scoville units.)

The following description was written by a police officer who sells pepper spray on his website. It is about his first experience being sprayed during a training exercise.

"It felt as if two red-hot pieces of steel were grinding into my eyes, as if someone was blowing a red-hot cutting torch into my face. I fell to the ground just like all the others and started to rub my eyes even though I knew better not too. The heat from the pepper spray was overwhelming. I could not resist trying to rub it off of my face. The pepper spray caused my eyes to shut very quickly. The only way I could open them was by prying them open with my fingers. Everything that we had been taught about pepper spray had turned out to be true. And everything that our instructor had told us that we would do, even though we knew not to do it, we still did. Pepper spray turned out to be more than I had bargained for."

As I tried to find my way down Sixth Street after the tear gas and pepper spray, I couldn't see. The person who found and guided me was Anita Roddick, the founder of the Body Shop, and probably the only CEO in the world who wanted to be on the streets of Seattle helping people that day. When your eyes fail, your ears take over. I could hear acutely. What I heard was anger, dismay, shock. For many people, including the police, this was their first direct action. Demonstrators who had taken non-violence training were astonished at the police brutality. The demonstrators were students, their professors, clergy, lawyers, and medical personnel. They held signs against dictatorship in Burma and violence. They dressed as butterflies.

The Seattle Police had made a decision not to arrest people on the first day of the protests (a decision that was reversed for the rest of the week). Throughout the day, the affinity groups created through the Direct Action Network stayed together. Tear gas, rubber bullets, and pepper spray were used so frequently that by late afternoon, supplies ran low. What seemed like an afternoon lull or standoff was because police had used up all their stores. Officers combed surrounding counties for tear gas, sprays, concussion grenades, and munitions. As police restocked, the word came down from the White House to secure downtown Seattle or the WTO meeting would be called off. By late afternoon, the Mayor and Chief announced a 7 p.m. curfew, "no protest" zones, and declared the city under civil emergency. The police were fatigued and frustrated. Over the next seven hours and into the night, the police turned downtown Seattle into Beirut.

That morning, it was the police commanders that were out of control, ordering the gassing and pepper spraying and shooting of people protesting non-violently. By evening, it was the individual police officers who were out of control. Anger erupted, protestors were kneed and kicked in the groin, and police used their thumbs to grind the eyes of pepper-spray victims. A few demonstrators danced on burning dumpsters that were ignited by pyrotechnic tear-gas grenades (the same ones used in Waco). Taunting, jeering, protestors were defiant. Tear gas canisters were being thrown back as fast as they were launched. Drum corps marched using empty 5-gallon water bottles for instruments.

Despite their steadily dwindling number, maybe 1,500 by evening, a hardy number of protestors held their ground, seated in front of heavily armed police, hands raised in peace signs, submitting to tear gas, pepper spray, and riot batons. As they retreated to the medics, new groups replaced them. Every local channel covered the police riots live. On TV, the police looked absurd, frantic and mean. Passing Metro buses filled with passengers were gassed. Police were pepper spraying residents and bystanders. The Mayor went on TV that night to say, that as a protestor from the '60s, he never could have imagined what he was going to do next: call in the National Guard.

This is what I remember about the violence. There was almost none until police attacked demonstrators that Tuesday in Seattle. Michael Meacher, environment minister of the United Kingdom, said afterward, "What we hadn't reckoned with was the Seattle Police Department who single-handedly managed to turn a peaceful protest into a riot." There was no police restraint, despite what Mayor Paul Schell kept proudly assuring television viewers all day. Instead, there were rubber bullets, which Schell kept denying all day. In the end, more copy and video was given to broken windows than broken teeth.

During that day, the anarchist black blocs were in full view. Numbering about one hundred, they could have been arrested at any time but the police were so weighed down by their own equipment, they literally couldn't run. The police had been apprised about the anarchists' intentions for months prior to the WTO conference. The Eugene Police had volunteered information and specific techniques to handle the black blocs, but had been rebuffed by the Seattle Police. It was widely known they would be there, and that they had property damage in mind. To the credit of the Mayor, the Police Chief, and the Seattle press, distinctions were consistently made between the bulk of the protestors and the so-called anarchists (later joined by local vandals as the night wore on). But the anarchists were not primitivists, nor were they all from Eugene. They were well organized, and they had a plan.

The black blocs came with tools (crowbars, hammers, acid-filled eggs) and hit lists. They knew they were going after Fidelity Investments but not Charles Schwab. Starbucks but not Tully's. The GAP but not REI. Fidelity Investments because they are large investors in Occidental Petroleum, the oil company most responsible for the violence against the U'wa tribe in Colombia. Starbucks because of their non-support of fair-traded coffee. The GAP because of their sweathsops in Asia and the Fisher family's purchase of Northern California forests. They targeted multinational corporations which they see as benefiting from repression, exploitation of workers, and low wages. According to one anarchist group, the ACME collective:

> "Most of us have been studying the effects of the global economy, genetic engineering, resource extraction, transportation, labor practices, elimination of indigenous autonomy, animal rights and human rights and we've been doing activism on these issues for many years. We are neither ill-informed nor inexperienced."

They don't believe we live in a democracy, do believe that property damage (windows and tagging primarily) is a legitimate form of protest, and that it is not violent unless it harms or causes pain to a person. For the black blocs, breaking windows is intended to break the spells cast by corporate hegemony, an attempt to shatter the smooth exterior facade that covers corporate crime and violence. That's what they did. And what the media did is what I just did in the last two paragraphs: Report on the desires and recount the property damage caused by a tiny sliver of the 40-60,000 marchers and demonstrators.

Compare the pointed lawlessness of the anarchists with the carefully considered ability of the WTO to flout laws of sovereign nations. When the "The Final Act Embodying the Results of the Uruguay Round of Multilateral Trade Negotiations" was enacted April 15th, 1994 in Marrakesh, Morocco, it was recorded as a 550-page agreement that was then sent to Congress for passage. Ralph Nader offered to donate $10,000 to any charity of a congressman's choice if any of them signed an affidavit saying they had read it and could answer some basic questions about it.

Only one congressman—Sen. Hank Brown, a Colorado Republican—took him up on it. After reading the document, Brown changed his opinion and voted against the Agreement. There were no public hearings, dialogue, or education. What passed is an Agreement that gives the WTO the ability to overrule or undermine international conventions, acts, treaties, and agreements. The WTO directly violates "The Universal Declaration of Human Rights" adopted by member nations of the United Nations. (The proposed draft agenda presented in Seattle went further in that it would require Multilateral Agreements on the Environment such as the Montreal Protocol, the Convention on Biological Diversity, and the Kyoto Protocol to be in alignment with and subordinate to WTO trade polices.) The final Marrakesh Agreement contained provisions of which most of the delegates, even the heads of country delegations, were not aware, statutes that were drafted by sub-groups of bureaucrats and lawyers, some of whom represented transnational corporations.

The police mandate to clear downtown was achieved by 9 p.m. Tuesday night. But police, some who were fresh recruits form outlying towns, didn't want to stop there. They chased demonstrators into neighborhoods where the distinctions between protestors and citizens vanished. The police began attacking bystanders, witnesses, residents, and commuters. They had completely lost control. When President Clinton sped from Boeing airfield to the Westin Hotel at 1:30 a.m. Wednesday, his limousines entered a police-ringed city of broken glass, helicopters, and boarded windows. He was too late. The mandate for the WTO had vanished sometime that afternoon.

The next morning, and over the next days, a surprised press corps went to work and spun webs. They vented thinly veiled anger in columns, and pointed guilt-mongering fingers at brash, misguided white kids. They created myths, told fables. What a majority of media projected onto the marchers and activists, in an often-contradictory manner, was that the protesters are afraid of a world without walls; that they want the WTO to have even more rules; that anarchists led by John Zerzan from Eugene ran rampant; that they blame the WTO for the world's problems; that they are opposed to global integration; that they are against trade; that they are ignorant and insensitive to the world's poor; that they want to tell other people how to live. The list is long and tendentious.

Patricia King, one of two *Newsweek* reporters in Seattle, called me from her hotel room at the Four Seasons and wanted to know if this was the '60s redux. No, I told her. The '60s were primarily an American event; the protests against the WTO are international. Who are the leaders? she wanted to know. There are no leaders in the traditional sense. But there are thought leaders, I said. Who are they? she asked. I began to name some, including their writings, area of focus, and organizational affiliations: Martin Khor of the Third World Network in Malaysia, Vandana Shiva from India, Walden Bello of Focus on the Global South, Maude Barlow of the Council of Canadians, Tony Clarke of Polaris Institute, Jerry Mander of the International Forum on Globalization (IFG), Susan George of the Transnational Institute, David Korten of the People-Centered Development Forum, John Cavanagh of the Institute for Policy Studies, Lori Wallach of Public Citizen, Mark Ritchie of the Institute For Agriculture and Trade Policy, Anuradha Mittal of Institute for Food & Development Policy, Helena Norberg-Hodge of the International Society for Ecology and Culture, Owens Wiwa of the Movement for the Survival of the Ogoni People, Chakravarthi Raghavan of the Third World Network in Geneva, Debra Harry of the Indigenous Peoples Coalition Against Biopiracy, José Bové of the *Confederation Paysanne Europèenne*, Tetteh Hormoku of the Third World Network in Africa, Randy Hayes of Rainforest Action Network. Stop, stop, she said. I can't use these names in my article. Why not? Because Americans have never heard of them. Instead, *Newsweek* editors put the picture of the Unabomber, Theodore Kaczynksi, in the article because he had, at one time, purchased some of John Zerzan's writings.

Some of the mainstream media also assigned blame to the protesters for the meeting's outcome. But ultimately, it was not on the streets that the WTO broke down. It was inside. It was a heated and rancorous Ministerial, and the meeting ended in a stalemate, with African, Caribbean, and some Asian countries refusing to support a draft agenda that had been negotiated behind closed doors without their participation. With that much contention inside and out, one can rightly ask whether the correct question is being posed. The question, as propounded by corporations, is how to make trade rules more uniform. The proper question, it seems to me, is how do we make trade rules more differentiated so that different cultures, cities, peoples, places, and countries benefit the most. Arnold Toynbee wrote in 1871 that "Civilizations in decline are consistently characterized by a tendency toward standardization and uniformity. Conversely, during the growth stage of civilization, the tendency is toward differentiation and diversity."

Those who marched and protested opposed the tyrannies of globalization, uniformity, and corporatization, but they did not necessarily oppose internationalization of trade. Economist Herman Daly has long made the distinction between the two. Internationalization means trade between nations. Globalization refers to a system where there are uniform rules for the entire world, a world in which capital and goods move at will without the rule of individual nations. Nations, for all their faults, set trade standards. Those who are willing to meet those standards can do business with them. Do nations abuse this? Always and constantly; the U.S. being the worst offender. But nations do provide, where democracies prevail, a means for people to set their own policy, to influence decisions, and determine their future. Globalization supercedes the nation, the state, the region and the village. While eliminating nationalism is indeed a good idea, the elimination of sovereignty is not.

One recent example of the power of the WTO is Chiquita Brands International, a $2-billion-dollar corporation which recently made a large donation to the Democratic Party. Coincidentally, the United States filed a complaint with the WTO against the European Union because European import policies favored bananas coming from small Caribbean growers instead of the banana conglomerates. The Europeans freely admitted their bias and policy: they restricted imports from large multinational companies in Central America (plantations whose lands were secured by U.S. military force during the past century), and favored small family farmers from former colonies who use fewer chemicals. It seemed like a decent thing to do, and everyone thought the bananas tasted better. For banana giants, such as Chiquita, this was untenable.

The United States prevailed in this WTO-arbitrated case. So who really won, and who lost? Did the Central American employees at Chiquita Brands win? Ask the hundreds of workers in Honduras who were made infertile by the use of dibromo-chloropropane on the banana plantations. Ask the mothers whose children have birth defects from pesticide poisoning. Did the shareholders of Chiquita win? At the end of 1999, Chiquita Brands was losing money because they were selling bananas under cost to muscle their way into the European market. Their stock was at a 13-year low, the shareholders were angry, the company was up for sale, but the prices of bananas in Europe are really cheap. Who lost? Carribean farmers who could formerly make a living and send their kids to school can no longer do so because of low prices and demand.

Globalization leads to the concentration of wealth inside large multinational corporations such as Time-Warner, Microsoft, GE, Exxon and Wal-Mart. These giants can obliterate social capital and local equity, and create cultural homogeneity in their wake. Countries as different as Mongolia, Bhutan, and Uganda will have no choice but to allow Blockbuster, Burger King, and Pizza Hut to operate within their borders. Under WTO, even decisions made by local communities to refuse McDonald's entry (as did Martha's Vineyard) could be overruled. The as yet unapproved draft agenda calls for WTO member governments to open up their procurement process to multi-national foreign corporations. No longer could local governments buy preferentially from local vendors. It could force governments to essentially privatize health and allow foreign companies to bid on delivering national health care programs. It could privatize and commodify education, or ban cultural restrictions to entertainment, advertising, or commercialism as a trade barrier. In addition, globalization kills self-reliance, since smaller local businesses can rarely compete with highly capitalized firms who seek market share instead of profits. Thus, developing regions may become more subservient to distant companies, with more of their income exported rather than being spent locally.

On the weekend prior to the WTO meeting, the International Forum on Globalization held a two-day teach-in at Benaroya Hall in downtown Seattle on just such questions of how countries can maintain autonomy in the face of globalization. Chaired by IFG President Jerry Mander, more than 2,500 people from around the world attended. A similar number were turned away. It was the hottest ticket in town—but somehow that ticket did not get into the hands of pundits and columnists. It was an extravagant display of research, intelligence, and concern, expressed by scholars, diplomats, writers, academics, fishermen, scientists, farmers, geneticists, businesspeople, and lawyers. Beyond and before the teach-in, non-governmental organizations, institutes, public interest law firms, farmers organizations, unions, and councils had been issuing papers, communiqués, press releases, books, and pamphlets for years. They were almost entirely ignored by the WTO.

But something else was happening in Seattle underneath the debates and protests. In Stewart Brand's new book, *The Clock of the Long Now: Time and Responsibility*, he discusses what makes a civilization resilient and adaptive. Scientists have studied the same question about ecosystems. How does a system, be it cultural or natural, manage change, absorb shocks, and survive especially when change is rapid and accelerating? The answer has much to do with time, both our use of it and our respect for it. Biological diversity in ecosystems buffers against sudden shifts because different organisms and elements fluctuate at different time scales—flowers, fungi, spiders, trees, laterite, and foxes—

all have different rates of change and response. Some respond quickly, others slowly, so that the system, when subjected to stress, can move, sway, and give, and then return and restore.

The WTO was a clash of chronologies or time frames, at least three, probably more. The dominant time frame was commercial. Businesses are quick, welcome innovation in general, and have a bias for change. They need to grow more quickly than ever before. They are punished, pummeled and bankrupted if they do not. With worldwide capital mobility, companies and investments are rewarded or penalized instantly by a network of technocrats and money managers who move $2 trillion a day seeking the highest return on capital. The Internet, global communications, high-speed transportation and greed are all making businesses move faster than before.

The second time frame is culture. It moves more slowly. Cultural revolutions are resisted by deeper, historical beliefs. The first institution to blossom under perestroika was the Russian Orthodox Church. In 1989 I walked into a church near Boris Pasternak's dacha and heard priests and babushkas reciting the litany with perfect recall as if 72 years of repression had never happened. Culture provides the slow template of change within which family, community, and religion prosper. Culture provides identity and, in a fast-changing world of displacement and rootlessness, becomes ever more important. In between culture and business is governance, faster than culture, slower than commerce.

At the heart, the third and slowest chronology is earth, nature, the web of life. As ephemeral as it may seem, it is the slowest clock ticking, always there, responding to long, ancient evolutionary cycles that are beyond civilization.

These three chronologies often conflict. As Stewart Brand points out, business unchecked becomes crime. Look at Russia. Look at Microsoft. Look at history. What makes life worthy and allows civilizations to endure are all the things that have "bad" payback under commercial rules: infrastructure, universities, temples, poetry, choirs, literature, language, museums, terraced fields, long marriages, line dancing, and art. Most everything we hold valuable is slow to develop, slow to learn, and slow to change. Commerce requires governing by politics, art, culture, and nature, to slow it down, to make it heedful, to make it pay attention to people and place. It has never done this on its own. The extirpation of languages, cultures, forests, and fisheries is occurring worldwide in the name of speeding up business. Business itself is stressed out of its mind by rapid change.

The rate of change is unnerving to all, even to those who are benefiting. To those who are not benefiting, it is devastating. What marched in the streets of Seattle? Slower time strode into the WTO. Ancient identity emerged. The cloaks of the forgotten paraded on the backs of our children. What appeared in Seattle were the details, dramas, stories, peoples, and puppet creatures that had been ignored by the bankers, diplomats and the rich. Corporate leaders believe they have discovered a treasure of immeasurable value, a trove so great that surely we will all benefit. It is the treasure of unimpeded commerce flowing everywhere as fast as is possible. But in Seattle, quick time met slow time. The turtles, farmers, and priests weren't invited and don't need to be because they are the shadow world that cannot be overlooked, that will tail and haunt the WTO, and all it successors, for as long as it exists.

They will be there even if they meet in totalitarian countries where free speech is criminalized. They will be there in dreams of delegates high in the Four Seasons Hotel. They will haunt the public relations flacks who solemnly insist that putting the genes of scorpions into our food is a good thing. What gathered around the Convention Center and hotels was everything the WTO left behind. In the Inuit tradition, there is a story of a fisherman who trolls an inlet. When a heavy pull on the fisherman's line drags his kayak to sea, he thinks he has caught the "big one," a fish so large he can eat for weeks, a fish so fat that he will prosper ever after, a fish so amazing that the whole village will wonder at his prowess. As he imagines his fame and coming ease, what he reels up is Skeleton Woman, a woman flung from a cliff and buried long ago, a fish-eaten carcass resting at the bottom of the sea that is now entangled in his line. Skeleton Woman is so snarled in his fishing line that she is dragged behind the fisherman wherever he goes. She is pulled across the water, over the beach, and into his house where he collapses in terror. In the retelling of this story by Clarissa Pinkola Estes, the fisherman has brought up a woman who represents life and death, a specter who reminds us that with every beginning there is an ending, for all that is taken, something must be given in return, that the earth is cyclical and requires respect. The fisherman, feeling pity for her, slowly disentangles her, straightens her bony carcass, and finally falls asleep.

During the night, Skeleton Woman scratches and crawls her way across the floor, drinks the tears of the dreaming fisherman, and grows anew her flesh and heart and body. This myth applies to business as much as it does to a fisherman. The apologists for the WTO want more—engineered food, sleeker planes, computers everywhere, golf courses that are preternaturally green. They see no limits; they know of no downside. But Life always comes with Death, with a tab, a reckoning. They are each other's consorts, inseparable and fast. These expansive dreams of the world's future wealth were met with perfect symmetry by Bill Gates, Jr. the co-chair of the Seattle host committee, the world's richest man.

But Skeleton woman—the uninvited guest—also showed up in Seattle. And the illusion of wealth, the imaginings of unfettered growth and expansion, became small and barren in the eyes of the world. Dancing, drumming, ululating, marching in black with a symbolic coffin for the world, Skeleton woman wove through the sulphurous rainy streets of the night. She couldn't be killed or destroyed, no matter how much gas or pepper spray or rubber bullets were used. She kept coming back and sitting in front of the police and raising her hands in the peace sign, and was kicked, and trod upon, and it didn't make any difference. Skeleton Woman told corporate delegates and rich nations that they could not have the world. It is not for sale. The illusions of world domination have to die, as do all illusions. Skeleton Woman was there to say that if business is going to trade with the world, it has to recognize and honor the world, her life and her people. Skeleton Woman was telling the WTO that it has to grow up and be brave enough to listen, strong enough to yield, courageous enough to give.

Skeleton Woman has been brought up from the depths. She has regained her eyes, voice and spirit. She is about in the world and her dreams are different. She believes that the right to self-sufficiency is a human right; she imagines a world where the means to kill people is not a business but a crime, where families do not starve, where fathers can work, where children are never sold, where women cannot be impoverished because they choose to be mothers and not whores. She cannot see in any dream a time where a man holds a patent to a living seed, or animals are factories, or people are enslaved by money, or water belongs to a stockholder. Hers are deep dreams from slow time. She is patient. She will not be quiet or flung to sea anytime soon.

Using armored vehicles, tear gas—which even made the delegations staying in hotels queasy—and, on top of that, pepper gas. Brutal methods, dragging people through the streets. Six hundred arrested. What would happen if such behavior took place in Cuba? What would they say if they saw an army, the National Guard, occupying the city? Tons of masked men with horrifying outfits to scare people, thousands of police in all directions, men being dragged, horses and other animals to attack people? They would say that it was a flagrant and massive violation of human rights and that, therefore, they had to use the NATO formula to conduct a 'humanitarian' intervention.

Fidel Castro, receiving the
Cuban delegation upon its
return from Seattle

2

How We Really Shut Down the WTO

Starhawk

It's been two weeks now since the morning when I awoke before dawn to join the blockade that shut down the opening meeting of the WTO. Since getting out of jail, I've been reading the media coverage and trying to make sense out of the divergence between what I know happened and what has been reported.

For once in a political protest, when we chanted, "The whole world is watching!" we were telling the truth. I've never seen so much media attention on a political action. Most of what has been written is so inaccurate, however, that I can't decide if the reporters in question should be charged with conspiracy or incompetence. The reports have pontificated endlessly about a few broken windows, and mostly ignored the Direct Action Network (D.A.N.), the group that successfully organized the nonviolent direct action that ultimately involved thousands of people. The true story of what made the action a success is not being told.

The police, in defending their brutal and stupid mishandling of the situation, have said they were "not prepared for the violence." In reality, they were unprepared for the nonviolence and the numbers and commitment of the nonviolent activists—even though the blockade was organized in open, public meetings and there was nothing secret about our strategy. My suspicion is that our model of organization and decision making was so foreign to their picture of what constitutes leadership that they literally could not see what was going on in front of them. When authoritarians think about leadership, the picture in their minds is of one person, usually a guy, or a small group standing up and telling other people what to do. Power is centralized and requires obedience.

In contrast, our model of power was decentralized, and leadership was invested in the group as a whole. People were empowered to make their own decisions, and the centralized structures were for coordination, not control. As a result, we had great flexibility and resilience, and many people were inspired to acts of courage they could never have been ordered to do. Here are some of the key aspects of our model of organizing.

Training and Preparation

In the weeks and days before the blockade, thousands of people were given nonviolence training: a three-hour course that combined the history and philosophy of nonviolence with real life practice through role plays in staying calm in tense situations, using nonviolent tactics, responding to brutality, and making decisions together. Thousands also went through a second-level training in jail preparation, solidarity strategies and tactics and legal aspects. In addition, there were trainings in first-aid, blockade tactics, street theater, meeting facilitation and other skills.

While many more thousands of people took part in the blockade who had not attended any of these trainings, a nucleus of groups existed who were prepared to face police brutality and who could provide a core of resistance and strength. And in jail, I saw many situations that played out just like the role plays. Activists were able to protect members of their group from being singled out or removed by using tactics developed in the trainings. The solidarity tactics we had prepared became a real block to the functioning of the system.

Common Agreements

Each participant in the action was asked to agree to the non-violence guidelines: To refrain from violence, physical or verbal; not to carry weapons; not to bring or use illegal drugs or alcohol; and not to destroy property. We were asked to agree only for the purpose of the November 30 action—not to sign on to any of these as a life philosophy, and the group acknowledged that there is much diversity of opinion around some of these guidelines.

Affinity Groups, Clusters and Spokescouncils

The participants in the action were organized into small groups called affinity groups. Each group was empowered to make its own decisions around how it would participate in the blockade. There were groups doing street theater, others preparing to lock themselves to structures, groups with banners and giant puppets, others simply prepared to link arms and nonviolently block delegates. Within each group, there were generally some people prepared to risk arrest and others who would be their support people in jail, as well as a first aid person.

Affinity groups were organized into clusters. The area around the Convention Center was broken down into thirteen sections, and affinity groups and clusters committed to hold particular sections. As well, some groups were "flying groups"—free to move to wherever they were most needed. All of this was coordinated at spokescouncil meetings, where affinity groups each sent a representative who was empowered to speak for the group.

In practice, this form of organization meant that groups could move and react with great flexibility during the blockade. If a call went out for more people at a certain location, an affinity group could assess the numbers holding the line where they were and choose whether or not to move. When faced with tear gas, pepper spray, rubber bullets and horses, groups and individuals could assess their own ability to withstand the brutality. As a result, blockade lines held in the face of incredible police violence. When one group of people was finally swept away by gas and clubs, another would move in to take their place. Yet there was also room for those of us in the middle-aged, bad lungs/bad backs affinity group to hold lines in areas that were relatively peaceful, to interact and dialogue with the delegates we turned back, and to support the labor march that brought tens of thousands through the area at midday. No centralized leader could have coordinated the scene in the midst of the chaos, and none was needed—the organic, autonomous organization we had developed proved far more powerful and effective. No authoritarian figure could have compelled people to hold a blockade line while being tear gassed—but empowered people, free to make their own decisions, did choose to do that.

Consensus Decision Making

The affinity groups, clusters, spokescouncils and working groups involved with D.A.N. made decisions by consensus: a process that allows every voice to be heard and that stresses respect for minority opinions. Consensus was part of the nonviolence and jail trainings and we made a small attempt to also offer some special training in meeting facilitation. We did not interpret consensus to mean unanimity.

The only mandatory agreement was to act within the nonviolence guidelines. Beyond that, the D.A.N. organizers set a tone that valued autonomy and freedom over conformity, and stressed coordination rather than pressure to conform.

So, for example, our jail solidarity strategy involved staying in jail where we could use the pressure of our numbers to protect individuals from being singled out for heavier charges or more brutal treatment. But no one was pressured to stay in jail, or made to feel guilty for bailing out before the others.

We recognized that each person has their own needs and life situation, and that what was important was to have taken action at whatever level we each could. Had we pressured people to stay in jail, many would have resisted and felt resentful and misused. Because we didn't, because people felt empowered, not manipulated, the vast majority decided for themselves to remain in, and many people pushed themselves far beyond the boundaries of what they had expected to do.

Vision and Spirit

The action included art, dance, celebration, song, ritual and magic. It was more than a protest; it was an uprising of a vision of true abundance, a celebration of life and creativity and connection, that remained joyful in the face of brutality and brought alive the creative forces that can truly counter those of injustice and control.

Many people brought the strength of their personal spiritual practice to the action. I saw Buddhists turn away angry delegates with loving kindness. We Witches led rituals before the action and in jail, and called on the elements of nature to sustain us. I was given Reiki when sick and we celebrated Hanukkah with no candles, but only the blessings and the story of the struggle for religious freedom. We found the spirit to sing in our cells, to dance a spiral dance in the holding cell, to laugh at the hundred petty humiliations the jail inflicts, to comfort each other and listen to each other in tense moments, to use our time together to continue teaching and organizing and envisioning the flourishing of this movement. For me, it was one of the most profound spiritual experiences of my life.

I'm writing this for two reasons. First, I want to give credit to the D.A.N. organizers who did a brilliant and difficult job, who learned and applied the lessons of the last twenty years of nonviolent direct action, and who created a powerful, successful and life-changing action in the face of enormous odds, an action that has changed the global political landscape and radicalized a new generation.

Secondly, the true story of how this action was organized provides a powerful model that activists can learn from. Seattle was only a beginning. We have before us the task of building a global movement to overthrow corporate control and create a new economy based on fairness and justice, on a sound ecology and a healthy environment, one that protects human rights and serves freedom. We have many campaigns ahead of us, and we deserve to learn the true lessons of our successes.

In Seattle, the demonstrators were grappling with complex economic issues—globalization, protectionism, export trade, intellectual properties—issues the most sophisticated experts have had a hard time explaining. But through all of that complexity, a certain diamond-hard idea shone brightly: that the schemes of well-dressed men of finance and government gathering in ornate halls were dangerous to the health and lives of working people all over the world. Thousands in the streets, representing millions, showed their determination to resist these schemes.

In one crucial way, it was a turning point in the history of the movements of recent decades: a departure from the single-issue focus of the Seabrook occupation of 1977, the nuclear freeze rally in Central Park in 1982, and the gatherings in Washington for the Equal Rights Amendment in 1978, for lesbian and gay rights in 1993, for the Million Man March in 1995, and for the Stand for Children in 1996. This time, the union movement was at the center. The issue of class—rich and poor, here and all over the globe—bound everyone together.

It was, at the least, a flash of the possible. It recalled the prophecy of A. Philip Randolph in November of 1963, speaking to an AFL-CIO convention shortly after the civil rights march brought 200,000 people, black and white, to the nation's capital. Randolph told the delegates: "The Negro's protest today is but the first rumbling of the underclass. As the Negro has taken to the streets, so will the unemployed of all races take to the streets."

There will be more rumblings to come.

Howard Zinn, author of *A People's History of the United States*

3

The Revolt of the Globalized

Luis Hernandez Navarro

The 21st century did not begin on November 9, 1989, with the fall of the Berlin Wall. Nor did it begin on the first of January of the year 2000. The new century was born on November 30, 1999 with the revolt of the globalized in Seattle, Washington.

The boycott of the opening of the World Trade Organization summit—staged by 50,000 demonstrators—is not the last protest by the forgotten of the earth, but rather the great premiere in "society" of world resistance to a globalization model being led by transnational coalitions. Ecologists, farmers from the First World, unionists, gay rights activists, NGOs supporting development, feminists, punks, human rights activists, representatives of indigenous peoples, the young and not young, people from the United States, Canada, Europe, Latin America, Europe and Asia—all unleashed a peaceful protest against the new Babylon.

Beyond their national diversity or their political differences, the demonstrators share their rejection of the slogan "All power to the transnational corporations!" present on the free trade agenda in the abstract. They believe that an ideological alibi is concealed behind the worship of God–Market–creator–of–the–society–of–the–future: an ideology that is trying to limit social victories, levels of well-being, environmental standards and the range of intervention of national policies, for the benefit of the great financial capital.

Behind the Seattle protest, there is a convergence of planetary networks and coalitions, built throughout the last two decades. In the United States, for example, the struggle against GATT, against NAFTA with Canada and with Mexico, and against the Initiative of the Americas, has a long organizing tradition that goes far beyond the traditional 'protectionist' logic. Its origins go back to the effective boycott organized against Nestle in the early seventies. Its second moment came during the opposition to GATT. Many groups of agriculturists, environmentalists and consumers in that country considered the Uruguay Round of 1985–1986—promoted by the Reagan administration—to be a government maneuver for achieving reform in agricultural policies through international negotiations (reduction of subsidies) that could not be achieved within the United States. Broad international coalitions were built during this struggle, with organizations of rural producers in Europe and Japan, who form the backbone of the new mobilizations.

In many industrialized countries, international commercial agreements, without checks and without compensation policies, are seen by many citizens as an instrument that allows international bureaucracies associated with the large corporations to mock the social controls won over years of struggle. Modern computer networks, the proliferation of hundreds of NGOs and the ease in moving about the world have made possible the formation of pockets of resistance which transcend national boundaries and which have created a new internationalism.

The mobilizations against the WTO in Seattle had been preceded by hundreds of new struggles of a new kind all over the world. In 1999, a French farmer destroyed a McDonald's in his community, in order to protest against the food degradation promoted by this franchise. The conflict attained national visibility and achieved international notoriety. Its main protagonist, a believer in self-management and an old activist from the movement of 1968, became a modern campesino hero. In India, hundreds of rural men have burned the fields where Monsanto is experimenting with transgenic cotton, while thousands more have taken over the facilities of the Cargill seed marketer. The trade in genetically modified organisms has brought about an avalanche of commercial disputes. Indigenous organizations in South America have won legal suits against attempts to patent life forms. Hundreds of personalities and organizations have participated in the *encuentros* against neoliberalism convened by zapatismo.

The destruction of the old Nation-State, the creation on a large scale of millions of the newly excluded and the ideology of neoliberal globalization have produced a new transnational political actor: the globalized. The Revolt of Seattle is an announcement that his—and her—hour has arrived.

*L*atin America is a key battleground for world trade and the deals of the future. Former U.S. President Ronald Reagan used to talk about his vision of a huge free-trade zone from Alaska to Tierra del Fuego. So far, the North American Free Trade Agreement (NAFTA) includes Canada, the U.S. and Mexico in a treaty for free trade in goods and services.

Negotiations are underway to include the entire region in the Free Trade Area of the Americas (FTAA). These hemispheric talks are a potential blueprint for a global trade deal.

But there has been growing outrage from the Latin American left and right over the way the leaders of the WTO—a handful of powerful countries among 135 members—conduct their business.

Linda Diebel
Toronto Star

4

We Traveled to Seattle
A Pilgrimage of Transformation

Ken Butigan

Seattle proved to be the last great pilgrimage of the twentieth century. Aside from the occasional fealty and homage paid by e-pilgrims to the geeky founders of Microsoft, Amazon, and Starbucks, Seattle hardly resembles what is typically taken to be a pilgrimage site in a traditional sense. While rife with abundant charm, the self-described Emerald City perched on the cusp of the Pacific Rim is no Jerusalem, Rome, Machu Pichu or Benares. But then again, pilgrimage itself has undergone a profound transformation in the last hundred years. While millions still swell Mecca, Lourdes, and the cities dotting the Ganges every year, another form of "sacred journey" emerged in the twentieth century with as much or even more power. Those who traveled to Seattle in late November 1999 to protest the World Trade Organization consciously or unconsciously participated in this new and potent form of pilgrimage.

A Pilgrimage for Our Times

This "modern pilgrimage" was paradigmatically defined by Gandhi's 1930 march to the sea. This stalwart procession challenged the British monopoly on salt and, more importantly, defied imperial rule once and for all. Here was a bold public ritual in which spirituality and politics were dramatically and unmistakably interwoven. This 261-mile politico-religious pilgrimage was a sojourn from bondage to freedom palpably symbolized in practical, corporeal, kinesthetic actuality. These were real, live human beings mobilizing the most powerful symbol at their disposal—their inspirited bodies—in loving and relentless resistance. Theirs was literally a movement: a restless journey to the ocean and, eventually, to liberation.

Since Gandhi's pilgrimage, others have followed in the Mahatma's footsteps. We recall Martin Luther King, Jr.'s pilgrimage in 1965 from Selma to Montgomery to demand voting rights for African Americans, and the *peregrinacion* that Cesar Chavez led from Delano to Sacramento in 1966 to call for economic justice and dignity for California's migrant poor. There have been numerous other pilgrimages around the world demanding an end to violence and injustice, including many concerted journeys to the Nevada Test Site and other atomic proving grounds on the ancient land of indigenous peoples.

Then there are the other pilgrimages: pilgrimages of remembrance, of reckoning, and occasionally of healing. The survivors of the Holocaust who journey to Auschwitz. African American pilgrims who cross the ocean to see with their own eyes the embarkation points on the West Coast of Africa where slaves were dispatched to America. Japanese-Americans who travel to the Manzanar and Tule Lake concentration camps where Japanese-Americans were imprisoned in World War II. The U.S. veterans who stand brooding before the Vietnam Wall in Washington.

The Pilgrimage to Seattle

"Pilgrims," Richard R. Niebuhr writes, "are persons in motion—passing through territories not their own—seeking something we might call completion." James Preston speaks of pilgrimage as "spiritual magnetism." In more traditional terms, Jean and Wallace Clift point out that there are many different reasons that pilgrims set out on their journey: to hope and ask for a miracle; to give thanks; to achieve pardon; to answer an inner call; to experience a place of power; to express love of God; to reclaim lost or abandoned or forgotten parts of ourselves; to prepare for death; or to get outside the normal routine of life so something new can happen.

Pilgrimage, in short, is an actively mobilized process of bearing witness to woundedness and to the mysterious possibilities of sacredness.

Tens of thousands of people journeyed to Seattle to protest the injustice of the WTO and the perils it poses to indigenous societies, labor standards, human rights, civil liberties and environmental integrity. While these concerns were largely expressed in political and sociological terms, I would interpret them as ultimately deeply cultural and, even more, profoundly spiritual.

Taken as a whole, the dizzying events that transpired in Seattle represent many of the motivations for pilgrimage listed above. These "modern pilgrims" were drawn—almost magnetically, as Preston would phrase it—to a place that momentarily intersected with history and challenged its crushing inevitability. The urgency of this journey came from a deep intuition that the great web of violence in which we are caught today is spun by large economic and political forces, and that the instructions for this "web design" for the next decades were about to be codified in a very few short days on the shores of Puget Sound.

It is not enough to view this as ideological or a form of political analysis. In fact, we "traveled to Seattle" to defamiliarize the familiar, to ask for pardon, to reclaim lost parts of ourselves, to express gratitude that we have one another and the earth, to show love for a God whose name is Justice and Compassion and who longs for the Beloved Community, and to hope—and ask for—a miracle.

And what did we get? The December 3 headline of the *San Jose Mercury News* read: "Protests' power to alter public awareness." The banner of the top story in the Sunday edition of *Los Angeles Times* on December 5 declared, "WTO is Humbled, Changed Forever by Outside Forces." These are very preliminary judgments, but they signal the way in which the juggernaut of globalization has, at the very least, been problematized. There is an ambiguity attached to so-called "free trade" in a way that was not true a very short time ago. The events in Seattle broke the spell of the inevitability and unquestioned authority of global capital, and this in turn has laid the groundwork for a process of social and cultural transformation which has the potential to make the world more just, more ecologically sensitive, and ultimately a more peaceful place.

Pilgrimage of Nonviolent Change

Martin Luther King, Jr. entitled one of his essays the "Pilgrimage to Nonviolence." In spite of the impression left by much of the media coverage, 99.98 percent of the people who participated in the Seattle activities echoed King's "nonviolent pilgrimage" in word and deed. Sadly, this was not the case with the Seattle police—who created an unnecessarily provocative and confrontational atmosphere with unprovoked attacks on peaceful demonstrators—and a relatively small group of vandals who broke windows and spray-painted graffiti on storefronts and sidewalks. Countless others exercised nonviolence and thus symbolically embodied the heart of the pilgrimage required to change ourselves and the world: the journey in which we as individuals and as a people recognize our own woundedness and sacredness so that we can see, and respond to, the woundedness and sacredness of the other. In such a journey of love and courage, neither self-righteousness nor violence has a place.

A Pilgrim Future

The word pilgrim comes from the Latin legal word *pelegrinus*, meaning a "stateless person" or a person without a country. It has the connotation of one who "journeys between states." As we struggle to understand and live out interdependence without succumbing to the seduction and trap of the monoculture that "globalization" promises, perhaps this sense of pilgrimage—as a transformation beyond either nationalism or corporate integration—can fruitfully illuminate the journey we are called to undertake together in the coming century.

5

Seattle Debacle:
Revolt of the Developing Nations

Martin Khor

I t was an amazing week in Seattle. The WTO Ministerial Conference that was supposed to launch a new Round of trade negotiations collapsed suddenly, in almost total chaos, like a house of cards.

There is no new Round, no Seattle Declaration, not even a brief joint statement to thank the hosts or decide on the follow-up process.

In the aftermath of the collapse, there will be many theories and analyses on what happened. Some will focus on the protests by civil society groups representing labor, environment, consumer, pro-poor and Third World concerns. There were also the "direct action" activists that blocked delegates' access to the Opening Ceremony, which was then cancelled.

The main message of the protestors was heard loud and clear: that the WTO has gone much too far in setting global rules that "lock in" the interests of big corporations at the expense of developing countries, the poor, the environment, workers and consumers. The impact of grassroots protests against globalization, already evident in the campaigns on the multilateral agreement on investment (MAI) and against genetic engineering, had its coming-of-age in the street battles of Seattle.

Some will also pinpoint the inability of the U.S. and EU to bridge their differences as the immediate cause of the collapse.

This was of course a significant factor. The two giants of the trade system were striving for a compact in which the EU would agree to significantly reduce their agriculture subsidies, and in return the U.S. would agree to start negotiations on new issues like investment and competition.

As a last chip, the EC also threw its support to the U.S. to form a WTO working group on biotechnology, but this fell foul of the European Environment Ministers who objected to the EC's move, for which they said the EC had no mandate. This open spat between the EC and the Ministers further muddied the last-ditch attempt of the EU and U.S. to agree to a new Round.

However, the more basic cause of the Seattle debacle was the untransparent and undemocratic nature of the WTO system, the blatant manipulation of that system by the major powers, and the refusal of many developing countries to continue to be on the receiving end.

The seeds of the North-South battle were sown in Geneva in the weeks before Seattle. Developing countries voiced their disillusionment that five years after the WTO's creation they had not seen any benefits. Worse, the poor countries face potentially enormous dislocation when they implement their obligations arising from the WTO's many agreements.

They put forward dozens of proposals to resolve the "problems of implementation" of the WTO agreements, including changing some of the rules. But most of their demands were dismissed by the major powers that instead pushed for their own proposals to further empower the WTO through introducing new areas such as investment, competition, government procurement, labor and environmental standards.

The developing countries in general opposed these new issues which they saw would open up their markets further to the rich nations' big companies, or would give these rich nations new protectionist tools to block Third World products from entering northern markets.

Worse yet, the WTO Secretariat was used by the major powers to engage in untransparent procedures, such as holding informal meetings on crucial issues in small groups to which most developing countries were not invited. These so-called "Green Room" meetings infuriated the Third World Members of the WTO.

At Seattle, in contradiction to her promise to run a transparent meeting, the U.S. Trade Representative Charlene Barshefsky presided over a totally undemocratic process. She announced on the second day her "right" as chairman to use procedures of her own choosing to get a Declaration out of the meeting, a statement that infuriated the developing country delegations.

Barshefsky and the WTO Director-General Mike Moore set up several "Green Room" meetings, some running simultaneously, on key issues of disagreement. Only ten or twenty countries (the major powers plus a few selected developing countries) were invited to a typical Green Room meeting.

The plan of the organizers was to get the major powers (mainly the U.S. and EU) to agree among themselves, then apply pressure in the Green Rooms on a few influential developing countries to go along, and then pull together a Declaration to launch a new Round which all Members would be coerced to accept in a special meeting on the last day.

The vast majority of developing countries were shut out of the whole Green Room process. They were not even informed which meetings were going on or what was being discussed. Ministers and senior officials of most developing countries were left hanging around in the corridors or the canteen, trying to catch snippets of news or negotiating texts.

Their anger at the insult of being at the receiving end of such shabby treatment boiled over on the third day of the Conference. The African Ministers issued a strong statement that there was "no transparency" in the meeting, that African countries were generally excluded on issues vital to their future, that they were concerned over the intention to produce a ministerial text at any cost. "Under the present circumstances, we will not be able to join the consensus required to meet the objectives of this Ministerial Conference." Similar statements were issued by the Caribbean Community Ministers and by some Latin American countries.

Barshefsky and Moore were thus faced with the prospect that if a draft Declaration were presented at a final session, there would be an explosion of protests and a rejection by developing nations. That would totally expose to the public and the world media the manipulative methods by which the Seattle Conference, and more seriously the WTO in general, had been run.

In the end, it was less embarrassing to decide to let the Seattle meeting collapse without attempting even a brief Declaration. But the breakdown took place so fast that Barshefsky at the final plenary did not even try to get the Ministers to adopt a formal statement on the procedures for follow up talks.

All that was left is a transcript of Barshefsky's off-the-cuff closing remarks, in which she admitted that "we found that the WTO has outgrown the processes appropriate to an earlier time... We needed a process which had a greater degree of internal transparency and inclusion to accommodate a larger and more diverse membership."

Does the Seattle debacle and Barshefsky's remarks give hope for reform to the WTO's decision-making system? That depends on whether the developing countries can now make use of the impasse to press for a democratic system, for example by abolishing the green-room process that belongs to the feudal age, and which ultimately sank Seattle.

The big powers will however try hard to cling to their privileges. Both Barshefsky and the EC Trade Commissioner Pascal Lamy announced that the WTO Director General had now been delegated with the authority to carry forward the Seattle process. Lamy even told the media that Mike Moore would report directly back to the Ministers.

The implication is that the post-Seattle negotiations would be led by the Director General, who is known to be biased in favor of the major powers, rather than the WTO's General Council, the majority of whose Members are developing countries.

Are the major powers setting up one more device to control

the post-Seattle process so that they can rebuild the house of cards in line with the same old global trade architecture? And will the developing countries, which never agreed to the Barshefsky-Lamy decision to put the already discredited Moore in the driver's seat, refuse to "join the consensus" and place the authority of the follow-up process with the General Council, where it appropriately belongs?

These will be some of the immediate issues when the battle of Seattle resumes in Geneva.

The time that the collapse of the WTO's agenda and timetable will buy must be used to allow this crucial questioning of whether more open markets, particularly for third world exports, equals more growth, equals less poverty. The evidence is mostly in the other direction; more trade has meant more global and national inequality and more rapacious use of the world's resources, resulting in increased environmental degradation."

Colin Hines

6

Fixing or Nixing the WTO

Susan George

The civic movement's success in Seattle is a mystery only to those who had no part in it. Throughout 1999, thanks primarily to the Internet, tens of thousands of people opposed to the World Trade Organization (WTO) united in a great national and international effort of organization. Anyone could have a front seat, anyone could take part in the advance on Seattle. All you needed was a computer and a rough knowledge of English.

The main rallying point was the StopWTO Round distribution list. This put people in touch with the whole movement and enabled them to get their names on other more specialized lists. Among the most useful were those of the Corporate European Observatory in Amsterdam—unbeatable on the links between lobbies of transnational firms and United States or European trade negotiators—and the Third World Network and its director, Martin Khor, with its detailed information on the positions of Southern governments and everything that was brewing at the WTO's Geneva headquarters. A number of institutions published regular information bulletins: the International Centre for Sustainable Trade and Development (ICSTD) in Geneva, the Institute of Agriculture and Trade Policy (IATP) in Minneapolis, and Focus on the Global South in Bangkok. Enthusiasts from various countries, like retired Canadian trucker Bob Olson, located and circulated vital items of information from all over the web.

Add to this the frequent Internet updates on national anti-WTO movements in Europe, Australia, Canada, the U.S. and India, and the slightly less frequent updates from Africa, Latin America and Asia, and you begin to have some idea of the volume of information available and the work of thousands of militants-turned-experts: conferences, symposiums and seminars, leaflets and articles, interviews and press releases.

Army of Equals

In France outstanding work was done by the *Association pour la taxation des transactions financières pour l'aide aux citoyens* (Attac), whose international meetings in June 1999—including a high-profile WTO element—were attended by delegations from 80 countries, and by *Coordination pour le contrôle citoyen de l'OMC* (CCC-OMC), which covers 95 organizations including the *Confédération paysanne*, *Droits Devant!*, the *Fédération des finances CGT*, and the FSU, and has the political support of the Greens, the *Ligue communiste révolutionnaire* (LCR) and the Communist Party.

In the international division of work prior to Seattle, Friends of the Earth in London had undertaken to gather signatures from 1,500 organizations in 89 countries calling for a moratorium on the trade negotiations and a complete review of the operation of the WTO with full citizen participation. Mike Dolan of Public Citizen, an organization founded by Ralph Nader in Washington, DC, had been busy on the ground in Seattle since the spring of 1999, locating and booking the venues that would be needed to accommodate a huge number of meetings. In San Francisco, the International Forum on Globalization was putting the finishing touches to its November 26–27 teach-in, at which speakers from all the continents addressed an enthusiastic audience of 2,800 crammed into the Benaroya Symphony Hall.

For months, thousands of people had followed training courses in non-violent protest organized by the Direct Action Network (D.A.N.) (a coalition of environmental and political activists). In the run-up to the WTO meeting, the D.A.N. headquarters at

420 East Denny Avenue, Seattle, had become the focus for an army of equals. Separate teams had been formed to take charge in each of the 13 sectors surrounding the conference center. Their members—most of them prepared to be arrested—were in place at 7 a.m. on the first day and blocked the opening session.

Artists had been working well in advance on huge puppets and models that lent a festive air to an otherwise deeply political event. Students from dozens of universities, including nearby Washington State University, returned in force to the political scene, concerned by the damage to the environment and the exploitation of third world workers and children (as a result, *inter alia*, of a campaign against sweatshops called Clean Clothes).

Even more surprising, in the light of recent U.S. history, was the Sweeney-Greenie alliance named after John Sweeney, the leader of the powerful trade union federation AFL-CIO, and the Greens. Ever since the Vietnam war, trade unionists and environmentalists had been on opposite sides of the political fence. For organized labor, ecology was synonymous with leftist policies and unemployment. They buried their differences, however, and made common cause against the WTO. For the first time pacifists and human rights campaigners, too, were disturbed by the harmful consequences of globalization and joined in the anti-WTO movement. *Via Campesina*, a network representing peasant movements in 65 countries, also had a date in Seattle. This coalition of the century was completed by many foreign delegations, the two largest being those from France and Canada.

In short, everyone was ready except the police, who looked like something out of Star Wars and acted in a way that was quite over the top. There is evidence, backed up by photos and videos, of police provocation, coercion and collusion with "anarchist elements" that were in fact simply hooligans and wreckers.

Whole districts and blocks of buildings, old people and children, were attacked with pepper spray and other (as yet unidentified) gases. Five hundred and eighty people were arrested, and many of them were roughed up and kept in solitary confinement for more than 48 hours in defiance of the U.S. Constitution.

Millennium Round Stillborn

Thanks to Washington's intransigence on agriculture and Europe's wish to add a raft of new items (investment, competition policy, environment, public contracts, etc.) to the agenda; thanks to the revolt of representatives of the South, outraged at being excluded from the negotiations; and finally, thanks to the protest movement, the Millennium Round was stillborn.

The WTO still has a mandate, however, under the decisions taken at the Morocco ministerial conference in 1994, to resume at any time discussions on agriculture and services, including health, education, and "environmental and cultural services," whatever that may mean. The TRIPS agreement on intellectual property is also to be reopened, including the patenting of living organisms.

The instant people got back from Seattle, they all had their two pennies worth to say on the theme "things will never be the same again." And it is true. It was a defining moment, a beginning, but we must build on it without delay because the forces of neoliberalism, humiliated and determined to get control back, will lose no time in regrouping. In other words, the popular movement may have gained time and scored a fine victory, but it has not yet got the moratorium and review it was seeking.

The European Commission is anxious to resume negotiations "between responsible people" who have not budged an inch on the principle of free trade and commerce in the service of the transnationals. They will meet again, if possible behind closed doors, and will make sure opponents do not get another media platform like Seattle.

The basic strategy vis-à-vis governments, the European Commission, the WTO itself and the transnationals must be to maintain vigilance, keep up the mobilization and pressure, and mount an offensive of counter-proposals with the ultimate objective of building genuine international democracy. This will call for a sustained collective effort, for discussion and action. It cannot be planned in every detail at this time.

It should nevertheless be possible to agree on some principles at once. Trade must have no place in areas such as health, education and culture in the broadest sense of the term. The case of hormone-fed beef is a perfect illustration of the WTO's refusal to exercise due precaution. So if there is any doubt as to the harmlessness of a product, the burden of proof must in future lie with the exporter. No living organism must be patentable and any country must be free to manufacture and distribute basic medicines in its own territory. Food safety and the integrity of peasant communities are more important than trade.

The proceedings of the WTO body for the settlement of disputes must be subject to recognized principles of international law: human rights, multilateral agreements on the environment, and the basic conventions of the International Labor Organization (ILO). There must be an end to the WTO's refusal to discriminate on the basis of processes and methods of production (PMPs): we must be free to give preference to products that have *not* been made by children or semi-slaves.

The question is how to break the sterile North-South deadlock on the social and environmental clauses? With a jealous eye to the only halfway effective bargaining counter they have—low wages and cheap, pollution-generating production methods—some Southern governments see the introduction of rules in these areas as a disguised form of protection. One idea worth exploring might be to devise a system for rewarding the countries that make the greatest efforts in the areas of labor and the environment, instead of penalizing them as we do now. No-one is suggesting that the same wages should be paid everywhere or that Laos should be treated in the same way as Luxembourg.

Thanks to World Bank and United Nations Development Programme statistics, we know a great deal about levels of material and human development worldwide. Suppose the ILO and the United Nations Environment Programme were to classify all countries at a given level of development—including the most advanced—according to the respect they show for labor law and for nature. The best, at each level, would be granted tariff preferences or even exemption from customs duties, while the products of the others would be taxed according to their classification. Such a system would allow a review of the hallowed most-favored-nation clause, which in fact favors nothing but a rush to the abyss.

Free marketeers, from *The Economist* to Alain Madelin, the French neoliberal deputy, generally accuse opponents of the WTO of being ignorant, unrepresentative, against the poor, and against rules and in favor of anarchy and the law of the jungle. In fact, it is precisely because they know what they are talking about that the NGOs and citizens' movements are against the WTO. Seattle has shown that the popular movement represents many things and many people. It is touching to see the sudden neoliberal concern with the fate of the poor in the South—not always well represented by their governments—but very few people have so far been discovered who enjoy working for a pittance in degrading conditions, who do not mind being unable to send their children to school or living in an environment that has been laid waste.

The popular movement is all for rules, but not the rules of the WTO in its present form. That is why, in the words of the militants, we shall have to "fix it or nix it."

The WTO is basically the first constitution based on the rules of trade and the rules of commerce. Every other constitution has been based on the sovereignty of people and countries. Every constitution has protected life above profits. But [the] WTO protects profits above the right to life of humans and other species.

Vandana Shiva

7

Prattle in Seattle
Media Coverage Misrepresented Protests

Seth Ackerman

As tens of thousands of protesters rallied in Seattle to shut down the opening session of the World Trade Organization meeting last December, mainstream media treated protesters' concerns with indifference and often contempt. That hostility translated into slanted coverage of both the demonstrations and the police reaction.

A *U.S. News & World Report* headline, "Hell No, We Won't Trade" summarized a recurring motif: "anti-trade" became a common—though wildly inaccurate—label for the demonstrators in mainstream coverage. "A guerrilla army of anti-trade activists took control of downtown Seattle today," a *Washington Post* article (12/1/99) began. ABC News reporter John Cochran (11/30/99) said Seattle had become a "home for protests against world trade." *Newsweek* (12/13/99) reported that activists "posted Web pages to educate their followers on the evils of foreign trade."

It should go without saying that virtually none of those who oppose the World Trade Organization are against world trade—any more than those who boycotted General Electric were against electricity. Indeed, one of the unions most militant in its support for the Seattle protests was the Longshoremen—dockworkers whose jobs are entirely dependent on trade.

Yet ABC anchor Jack Ford (12/1/99) assumed that everyone whose job involves trade supports the WTO, as he pitted the demonstrators against the city hosting them: "No American city exports as much, President Clinton was happy to point out today, which helps explain why a good many people in Seattle are angry—at the protesters and their very anti-trade message." Similarly, an Associated Press (11/28/99) report on the protesters' "farfetched" concerns claimed that "for every campaigner lying down on a sidewalk this week to protest the WTO's efforts to reduce trade barriers, there is a happily employed Seattleite whose job depends on free commerce."

NBC financial correspondent Mike Jensen (11/29/99) was enlisted on the eve of the WTO meeting to extol the benefits of free trade. Jensen concluded that "most experts say getting rid of trade barriers on both sides is a good thing for American workers and consumers. But no matter what comes out of this four-day meeting—and a lot of analysts don't think it will be much— world trade has such momentum, almost nothing can get in its way." Similarly, *Newsweek* (12/13/99) insisted that although "the images from the streets seemed to form a new face of protest" in America, "the reality is that global trade is going to march on in any event; human ambition and the Internet are seeing to that."

"A Stew of Grievances"

Even coverage that did attempt to describe the protesters' goals dealt with them in only the vaguest terms—and often at a level of generalization that rendered the descriptions inaccurate or meaningless. An *ABC News* story by correspondent Deborah Wang in Seattle failed to address the activists' concerns with anything more than platitudes:

> They are fighting for essentially the same issues they campaigned against in the '60s. Corporations, which they say are still exploiting workers in the Third World. Agribusiness is still putting small farmers out of work. Mining companies, still displacing peasants from the land…. But what is different is that, for these protesters, this single organization, the WTO has come to symbolize all that is wrong in the modern world.

More helpful than such generalities would have been a summary of some of the protesters' specific complaints: that the WTO has issued rulings forcing member countries to repeal specific laws that protect public health and the environment; that it proposes new rules limiting countries' freedom to regulate foreign corporate investors; and that its decisions are made in secret by unaccountable tribunals.

Instead, ABC's Peter Jennings commented that "it seems as though every group with every complaint from every corner of the world is represented in Seattle this week." When the conference ended (12/3/99), he remarked that "the thousands of demonstrators will go home, or on to some other venue where they'll try to generate attention for whatever cause that moves them."

U.S. News (12/13/99) dismissed the protesters as "causists and all-purpose agitators." The *Philadelphia Inquirer*'s William R. Macklin (12/5/99) referred to them as "the terminally aggrieved" with "a stew of grievances so confusing that they drowned any hope of broad public support." *U.S. News*' November 1 preview concluded that despite "up to 50,000 demonstrators" expected at the event, "for the moment, the movement against free trade seems to have little traction in the United States."

CBS Evening News explained some of the background on its November 29 broadcast, but obscured the core criticisms of the WTO. Dan Rather reported that the WTO had ruled on many environmental issues, but failed to explain that the WTO has ruled *against* environmental restrictions in every case that has come before it. Indeed, Rather's reference to the WTO's ruling on "fishing restrictions aimed at saving endangered species" might have misled viewers into thinking that the WTO was intervening *on behalf* of threatened animals, instead of ruling that such restrictions are an unacceptable restraint on trade.

U.S. News (12/13/99) claimed that "many demonstrators had only a vague notion of what the five-year-old WTO actually does." But often it seemed as though reporters and commentators were unclear on the organization's role. When Clyde

Prestowitz of the business-oriented Economic Strategy Institute disingenuously referred to the WTO as "a relatively weak international body," CNN anchor Bill Tucker (12/1/99) complacently concluded, "It would seem to be much ado about nothing."

"Duped" by Buchanan

The lack of understanding of the demonstrators' concerns was unsurprising, given how seldom the media spoke with them. When the police first started using tear gas against street blockades, CNN reporter Katherine Barrett (11/30/99) turned for comment to Jerry Jasinowski, president of the National Association of Manufacturers. Jasinowski confessed that he was "struck by how loopy some of the protesters were" and observed that they were "shouting a lot of crazy different messages."

Perhaps the single WTO opponent who received the largest amount of time on CNN to expound his views was Pat Buchanan, who was interviewed, one-on-one and at length, by *Inside Politics* anchor Judy Woodruff (11/30/99). Though right-wing nationalists did not appear to be an appreciable fraction of the actual protesters in Seattle's streets, the media seemed to anoint Buchanan as a major leader of the anti-WTO movement. *New York Times* columnist Thomas Friedman wrote (12/1/99) that "knaves like Pat Buchanan" had "duped" the demonstrators—"a Noah's ark of flat-earth advocates, protectionist trade unions and yuppies looking for their 1960s fix"—into protesting the WTO.

"What's driving [the protests]?" CNN political analyst Bill Schneider asked on *Inside Politics* (11/30/99). "Resentment of big business for its irresponsible behavior, a resentment shared by the left"—followed by a soundbite of AFL-CIO leader John Sweeney—"and the right"—followed by a soundbite of Pat Buchanan. This type of right/left "evenhandedness" concerning the protests did not appear to be justified by the actual composition of the anti-WTO movement.

Media outlets seemed unconcerned by Buchanan's ineptness as a representative of labor, environmental and human rights activists. (See *Extra!*, 5-6/96.) As co-host of CNN's *Crossfire* (7/3/

91), for example, Buchanan once grilled public-sector union leader Gerald McEntee—one of the labor officials present years later at the Seattle demos—on "the suicidal impulses of American unions":

> A lot of the jobs now have disappeared—they're gone. One reason, one complaint, is the pay of the United Auto Workers and the benefits…. Aren't you fellows committing suicide by yourselves?

Anarchists Smash, Police Respond

Perhaps mainstream news outlets' confusion concerning the protesters' composition and goals contributed to their often skewed coverage of the behavior of the Seattle police and National Guard. A continuing theme in news reports was that the use of tear gas and concussion grenades was an appropriate response to "violent" activists. ("Violence" was a term consistently applied to the breaking of windows, a questionable way of characterizing property crimes.)

CBS News anchor Dan Rather reported (12/1/99) that "the meeting of the World Trade Organization was thrown into turmoil by violent demonstrations that went on into last night. That brought on today's crackdown." A CNN report from Seattle (12/1/99) claimed that "as tens of thousands marched through downtown Seattle, [a] small group of self-described anarchists smashed windows and vandalized stores. Police responded with rubber bullets and pepper gas."

But the sequence of events described in these reports was wrong. As Detective Randy Huserik, a spokesperson for the Seattle police, confirmed, pepper spray had first been used against protesters engaged in peaceful civil disobedience. CNN anchor Lou Waters asked Huserik (11/30/99) why the chemical irritant was used:

> Waters: How would you characterize the nature of the threat today? Were police assaulted? Is that what precipitated this?

> Huserik: Well, a rather large group of protesters…were

determined to continue blocking public entrance and exit in access of some of the various venue sites. They were given a lawful order to disperse, which was ignored. Officers then announced that the Seattle police officers would deploy pepper spray if the crowd did not disperse. For those that remained, the pepper spray was deployed in order to disperse that crowd.

In retrospect, it's ironic that on the eve of the protests, *NBC News* (11/29/99) was hyping Seattle authorities' precautions against "a potential chemical or biological attack." Chemical agents were widely used in Seattle, but only by the police against protesters.

One eyewitness, nonviolence trainer Matt Guynn, distributed the following account of police brutality over the Internet:

> In one scene I witnessed this morning (at 8th Avenue and Seneca), police who had been standing behind a blockade line began marching in lock-step toward the line, swinging their batons forward, and when they reached the line they began striking the (nonviolent, seated) protestors repeatedly in the back. Then they ripped off the protestors' gas masks, and sprayed pepper spray at point-blank range into their eyes repeatedly. After spraying, they rubbed the protestors' eyes and pushed their fingers around on their lips to aggravate the effect of the spray. And after all THIS, they began striking them again with batons.... The police then were able to break up the line, and the protestors retreated to the steps of a nearby church for medical assistance.

The lack of condemnation of police tactics—especially their teargassing and pepper-spraying of peaceful protesters—was a striking feature of the coverage. "Thanks for joining us and good luck to you out there," CNN anchor Lou Waters told a Seattle police spokesperson (12/1/99) as police continued their crackdown on demonstrators. A front-page *Los Angeles Times* article on the protests (12/2/99) featured a subhead that read "Police Commended for Restraint." Yet the only source cited by the *Times* was Seattle police chief Norm Stamper, who praised the "professionalism, restraint and competence" of his forces.

Contrast that with this account from Seattle physician Richard DeAndrea, posted on the website emperors-clothes.com:

> The police were using concussion grenades. They were ... shooting tear gas canisters directly at protesters' faces. They were using rubber bullets. Some of the damage I saw from these rubber bullets took off part of a person's jaw, smashed teeth.... There are people who have been ... treated for plastic bullet wounds. Lots of tear gas injuries, lots of damage to [the] cornea, lots of damage to the eyes and skin.

One of the few mainstream media accounts that conveyed the brutality of the Seattle police was written by a local correspondent for the *Seattle Post-Intelligencer* (12/2/99), who himself was arrested during the police rampage. Kery Murakami reported that "three Seattle police officers slammed me to the pavement, handcuffed me and threw me into the van. I was charged with failing to disperse even though I showed them reporter's credentials and repeatedly said I was just covering a story."

A disturbing indication of mainstream media attitudes toward coverage of the WTO meeting came before the conference, when Disney/ABC's Seattle affiliate announced that it would "not devote coverage to irresponsible or illegal activities of disruptive groups," adding that "KOMO 4 News is taking a stand on not giving some protest groups the publicity they want ... . So if you see us doing a story on a disruption, but we don't name the group or the cause, you'll know why." In a revealing choice of words, news director Joe Barnes described civil disobedience as "illegally disrupting the commerce of the city."

This decision by a corporate-owned news outlet to explicitly ignore the messages of groups practicing civil disobedience underscores the importance of independent journalism. Organizers in Seattle made a priority of setting up an Independent Media Center (www.indymedia.org), which offered alternative news on the demonstrations and their issues in every format from Internet chatrooms to satellite TV feeds.

ABC News offered a backhanded compliment to the Independent Media Center in its December 5 broadcast, noting that "the meeting of the World Trade Organization was a turning point for the so-called independent media—small, partisan news organizations and individual reporters with political opinions they could never express in the mainstream media."

The media activists, correspondent Brian Rooney said, "got out a worldwide message about the working poor, endangered species and the power of the World Trade Organization." Perhaps alternative media wouldn't be needed to get such messages out if there weren't so many political opinions that you can never express in mainstream media.

> When the civil rights activists of the South in the early sixties put into practice the principle they called "Nonviolent Direct Action," they were able to make heretofore invincible power yield. What happened recently in Seattle was another working out of that principle.
>
> The strike, the boycott, the refusal to serve, the ability to paralyze the functioning of a complex social structure: these remain potent weapons against the most fearsome state or corporate power.
>
> Howard Zinn

8

The Debate Over Tactics

Medea Benjamin

The anti-World Trade Organization protests in Seattle represent a watershed event not only for the struggle against "free trade," but also for all progressive social movements in the United States. The labor, human rights, and environmental movements succeeded through militant direct action in shutting down the first day of the WTO conference. Our movement made democracy, human rights, labor and environmental issues central themes of the debate surrounding the talks. The protests turned the WTO from an obscure acronym into a household name for millions.

The Seattle protests have also led to a debate over the question of force and violence, in particular the appropriateness of breaking windows and other acts of property destruction. Since Global Exchange was one of the key organizers of the planned civil disobedience component of the protest, and since we have been both praised and criticized for coming out against the property destruction that took place in Seattle, we feel it is important to clarify our position on the tactics some protesters employed.

What do we think of the breaking of windows and other vandalism that took place in downtown Seattle? It is important to understand that at the center of the Seattle protest and its success was mass, nonviolent civil disobedience—the same tactic that built the Civil Rights movement, the United Farm Workers Union, and that has been developed by Greenpeace and many other organizations in the environmental movement. The mass, nonviolent protests in Seattle represented the culmination of a months-long process of coalition-building by organizations that did not initially all know, understand or trust each other. We got to know each other as we discussed the politics of trade and investment, and discussed strategies for confronting the WTO. We won mutual trust and respect as we debated tactics. We became one movement as we took classes in civil disobedience tactics, and laid the foundation for legal defense. That collective and democratic process made possible the unity among environmentalists, labor unionists and many others—groups who had not always worked so well together in the past.

After that long, collaborative and democratic process, a small number of protesters who had ignored, boycotted, or repudiated this movement's process took it upon themselves to break the sense of solidarity and collective cohesion reached by scores of organizations and thousands of individuals. In the most sectarian way, they put their small organizations up against a mass movement. We are far less concerned about the glass that they broke than about the sense of collective self-discipline that they attempted—but failed—to shatter. They apparently believe that they represent an elite that knows what is best for the people, and which can ignore the decisions of coalitions and the collective spirit and ethos of this renewed social movement. Whatever they call themselves, this is elitist, anti-democratic and anti-movement behavior.

We think it is unfair for a small, unrepresentative group to use a massive, peaceful protest as a venue for destructive actions that go against the wishes of the vast majority of protesters. Those who engaged in the breaking of windows and other types of property damage were a small fraction of the protesters. The majority of protesters came to Seattle with the understanding that they were participating in a peaceful protest. This is certainly true of the unions and the religious community, who turned out the majority of the marchers, and opposed any type of violence.

At the same time, we strongly disagree with the argument that it was "young, alienated anarchist youth," who should be held responsible for the violence in Seattle, as some in the media have suggested. It was the police who engaged in the real violence, and we rigorously condemn their unjustified use of force against peaceful protesters. Several groups of protesters, including Global Exchange's own staff, came to Seattle prepared to carry out dignified acts of civil disobedience and were prepared to risk arrest. We understood that blocking entrances to keep delegates away from the WTO meeting could well lead to our arrest. We were shocked and outraged, however, when instead of arresting us, the police unleashed a torrent of tear gas, pepper spray, concussion grenades and rubber bullets in what has rightly been called a police riot.

We are also extremely concerned about allegations of police brutality against protesters in jail. We call on the city of Seattle to launch an investigation into the brutal tactics used against peaceful protesters.

Are we condemning anarchists in general? Of course not: we know that people who call themselves by various names and labels—conservative, liberals, radicals, socialists, Christians, pacifists, anarchists—protested in Seattle against corporate power. We believe that whatever the labels, those of us who stand opposed to the WTO and to corporate rule—and stand for human rights, labor rights, and environmental justice—form part of a single rising movement. We should work together to build that movement, not use labels to discredit opponents. Many young activists have now been called "violent anarchists." We reject this approach as a kind of "red-baiting" of young activists in the movement. People who call themselves anarchists can be found on all sides of this debate. We reject argument by epithet, and believe we should argue out the principles and tactics of our common movement in the process of building on the success and momentum of Seattle.

While there are occasions in which the destruction of property furthers the cause of social justice and helps garner public support, this was not one of them. The Boston Tea Party was an example of property destruction—a shipment of tea—but it was done by a group that came together precisely for this purpose. When the Zapatistas rose up in 1994 and destroyed army posts and other symbols of a repressive state, it was after 10 years of organizing support within their indigenous communities. They also explained to the outside world that their armed uprising was a last resort and an act of self-defense. Members of the religious community in the U.S. have destroyed weapons of mass destruction to express their profound moral opposition to war. Indian farmers have destroyed Monsanto seeds to counter the multinational's attempts to control their food supply. And forest activists have destroyed the engines of bulldozers to prevent the clear-cutting of old growth forests. The list of tactically thoughtful and politically principled property destruction goes on and on.

It is not property destruction, per se, that we object to. We believe strongly, however, that such acts have to be grounded in strong community support, a requirement clearly not met in Seattle.

In one-on-one discussions with those who were engaged in breaking windows, Global Exchange activists found that we share many of the same views and objectives. But the tactical and strategic differences become questions of political principle. Will we build a mass movement through democratic and collective processes? Or will a small group attempt to foist its tactics—and the resulting repression—on the movement in the naive hope that intensified conflict will "bring on the revolution"?

On November 30th we found that the police, rather than arresting those who had violated local laws, chose instead to unleash tear gas, rubber bullets, and clubs on those who peacefully resisted. When some individuals who were not part of the organized blockade chose to break windows or in other ways destroy property, the police ignored them, while at the same time terrorizing and in subsequent days arresting nonviolent activists. Perhaps the authorities preferred to see property destroyed, knowing that it would discredit the movement?

The impact of people breaking windows, overturning trash bins and looting; roughing up WTO delegates, store employees and customers; and blanketing downtown Seattle with graffiti was negative in the eyes of the general public.

Many of the key organizers of the protest had interviews set up with national media that were cancelled at the last minute because the media preferred to cover "the anarchists." Those stories tended to give the impression that the "violence of the protesters in the streets was met with violence on the part of the police." This was not what really happened on the streets—since the attacks on peaceful protesters started before downtown stores were targeted—but this perception of "violent protesters, violent cops" remained. We do not gain any credibility with the mass of Americans when we allow ourelves to be portrayed as running amok in the streets.

Our most experienced and militant activists against corporate power were aware of this. French farmer José Bové, who led a demonstration against McDonald's on Monday and is famous for his militant anti-corporate actions in France, was furious when a window at McDonald's was smashed, and he got up on a van to plead with protesters to stay nonviolent. A garment worker from Mexico who was outside the Gap when some people made attempts to break the windows not only felt the attempted destruction would send a bad message, but feared that in a police crackdown she could be swept up and deported.

Furthermore, while most of the targets in Seattle were the outlets of multinational corporations, there were also small stores and public spaces—such as a children's carousel in a public square—that were vandalized.

The employees and customers of retail stores are not our enemies and we should not put them at risk. We at Global Exchange have led or been part of aggressive, citizen-based campaigns against some of the very targets of the window breaking. We were one of the spearheads of the Nike campaign; we are presently leading the Gap/Old Navy campaign; we are pressuring Starbucks to buy Fair Trade coffee; and we recently settled a lawsuit against

Nordstroms for labor abuses in Saipan. We are, however, very respectful of the retail employees of those companies. Breaking windows and other acts of destruction put their safety in jeopardy and make them afraid of us. On Monday, November 29, at a McDonald's protest, there were terrified employees inside the McDonald's, and they certainly are not our enemies. On Tuesday, employees of NikeTown were in the store as its windows were destroyed and smoke bombs were hurled inside. The customers of these businesses are not our enemies either.

At Global Exchange we are careful in our actions to tell the employees and customers that our problem is not with them but with corporate policies. We try not to alienate or frighten them, but to educate them and make them our allies. This is how we have built successful, mass campaigns that are forcing corporations to change some of their most abusive policies.

Let's keep our eyes on the prize: we want to change the structure and rules of the global economy. That will require a mass movement; acts that are perceived by the public as violent do not move us in that direction.

Our movement has to be based on messages of compassion, respect for the environment, justice and equality. It also has to be based on collaborative and democratic processes. If we stay positive, inclusive, and democratic, we have a truly historic opportunity to build a global movement for social justice.

While Global Exchange feels strongly about the issues discussed here, we also feel that this issue should be a topic of conversation, not a source of divisiveness. The violence of the World Trade Organization and its corporate beneficiaries are our true opponents. The struggles against these foes—not our internal disputes—demand most of our attention, our commitment, and our passion.

Section Two

Dealing with Diversity

Although the Seattle protests brought together a wide range of people, the crowds were predominantly white. If we are going to build a truly democratic movement to transform the global economy, we must grapple with questions about the composition of the movement and how it can open itself up to different sectors of the world's population.

In her poignant essay, "Where Was the Color in Seattle?" Betita Martinez raises tough questions in a comradely way and comes out with useful answers. She also poses questions that must be answered by the movement rather than by any one author.

Manning Marable, in "Seattle and Beyond: Making the Connection in the 21st Century," argues for AfricanAmericans being in the forefront of struggles to transform the global economy because it is in their self-interest to do so.

The Indigenous People's Caucus at the Seattle protests issued a Declaration that stands as one of the most thorough and trenchant critiques of how the neoliberal model promoted by the WTO, World Bank and International Monetary Fund destroys nature and destroys native peoples.

The "Unity Statement of Philippine Social Movements, Labor Groups, Peoples' Organizations and NGOs" is a model for how diverse groups can develop a unified critique that will appeal to large sections of the public.

9

Where Was the Color in Seattle?

Looking for reasons why the Great Battle was so white

Elizabeth (Betita) Martinez

"I was at the jail where a lot of protesters were being held and a big crowd of people was chanting 'This Is What Democracy Looks Like!' At first it sounded kind of nice. But then I thought: is this really what democracy looks like? Nobody here looks like me."

Jinee Kim

In the vast acreage of published analysis about the splendid victory over the World Trade Organization in Seattle, it is almost impossible to find anyone wondering why the 40–50,000 demonstrators were overwhelmingly Anglo. How can that be, when the WTO's main victims around the world are people of color? Understanding the reasons for the low level of color, and what can be learned from it, is absolutely crucial if we are to make Seattle's promise of a new, international movement against imperialist globalization come true.

Among those who did come for the WTO meeting were some highly informative third world panelists who spoke Monday, November 29 about the effects of WTO on health care and on the environment. They included activist-experts from Mexico, Malaysia, the Philippines, Ghana, and Pakistan. On Tuesday, at the huge rally on November 30 before the march, labor leaders from Mexico, the Caribbean, South Africa, Malaysia, India, and China spoke along with every major U.S. union leader (all white).

Rank-and-file U.S. workers of color also attended, from certain unions and locals in certain geographic areas. There were young African Americans in the building trades; blacks from Local 10 of the ILWU in San Francisco and Latinos from its Los Angeles local; Asian Americans from SEIU; Teamsters of color from eastern Washington state; members of the painters' union and the union of Hotel Employees and Restaurant Employees (H.E.R.E.). Latino/a farmworkers from the UFW and PCUN (Pineros and Campesinos del Noroeste) of Oregon also attended. At one point a miner from the South Africa Labor Network cried, "In the words of Karl Marx, 'Workers of the world, unite!' " The crowd of some 25,000 people cheered.

Among community activists of color, the Indigenous Environmental Network (IEN) delegation led by Tom Goldtooth conducted an impressive program of events with Native peoples from all over the U.S. and the world. A 15-member multi-state delegation represented the Southwest Network for Environmental and Economic Justice based in Albuquerque, which embraces 84 organizations primarily of color in the U.S. and Mexico; their activities in Seattle were binational.

Many activist youth groups of color came from California, especially the Bay Area, where they had been working on such issues as Free Mumia, affirmative action, ethnic studies, and right-wing legislation such as the Proposition 21 "youth crime" initiative. Seattle-based forces of color that participated actively included the Filipino Community Center and the International People's Assembly, which led a march on Tuesday despite being the only one denied a permit. The predominantly white Direct Action Network (D.A.N.), a huge coalition, brought thousands to the protest. But Jia Ching Chen of the Bay Area's Third Eye Movement was the only young person of color involved in DAN's central planning.

Seattle's 27-year old Centro de la Raza organized a Latino contingent in the labor march and local university groups, including MEChA (Movimiento Estudiantil Chicano de Aztlan), hooked up with visiting activists of color. Black activists who have been fighting for an African–American Heritage Museum and Cultural Center in Seattle were there. Hop Hopkins, an AIDS activist in Seattle, also black, made constant personal efforts to draw in people of color.

Still, the overall turnout of people of color from the U.S. remained around five percent of the total. In personal interviews, activists gave me several reasons for this. Some mentioned concern about the likelihood of brutal police repression. Other obstacles included: lack of funds for the trip, inability to be absent from work during the week, and problems in finding child care.

Yet several experienced activists of color in the San Francisco Bay Area who had even been offered full scholarships chose not to go. A major reason for not participating, and the reason given by many others, was lack of knowledge about the WTO. As one Filipina said, "I didn't see the political significance of it how the protest would be anti-imperialist. We didn't know anything about the WTO except that lots of people were going to the meeting." One of the few groups that did feel informed, and did participate, was the hip-hop group Company of Prophets. According to African- American member Rashidi Omari of Oakland, this happened as a result of their attending teach-ins by predominantly white groups like Art and Revolution. Company of Prophets, rapping from a big white van, was in the front ranks of the 6 a.m. march that closed down the WTO on November 30.

The problem of unfamiliarity with the WTO was aggravated by the fact that Black and Latino communities across the U.S. lack Internet access compared to many white communities. A July 1999 federal survey showed that among Americans earning $15,000-$35,000 a year, more than 32 percent of white families owned computers but only 19 percent of Black and Latino families had them. In that same income range, only 9 percent of African American and Latino homes had Internet access compared to 27 percent of white families. So information about WTO and all the plans for Seattle did not reach many people of color.

Limited knowledge meant a failure to see how the WTO affected the daily lives of U.S. communities of color. "Activists of color felt they had more immediate issues," said Rashidi. "Also, when we returned, people told me of being worried that family and peers would say they were neglecting their own communities, if they went to Seattle. They would be asked, 'Why are you going? You should stay here and help your people.' "

Along with such concerns about linkage came the assumption that the protest would be as overwhelmingly white as it was. Coumba Toure, a Bay Area activist originally from Mali, West Africa, said she had originally thought, "the whites will take care of the WTO, I don't need to go." Others were more openly apprehensive. For example, Carlos ("Los" for short) Windham of Company of Prophets told me, "I think even Bay Area activists of color who understood the linkage didn't want to go to a protest dominated by 50,000 white hippies."

People of color had reason to expect the protest to be white-dominated. Roberto Maestas, director of Seattle's Centro de la Raza, told me that in the massive local press coverage before the WTO meeting, not a single person of color appeared as a spokesperson for the opposition. "Day after day, you saw only white faces in the news. The publicity was a real deterrent to people of color. I think some of the unions or church groups should have had representatives of color, to encourage people of color to participate."

Four protesters of color from different Bay Area organizations talked about the "culture shock" they experienced when they first visited the "Convergence," the protest center set up by the Direct Action Network, a coalition of many organizations. Said one, "When we walked in, the room was filled with young whites calling themselves anarchists. There was a pungent smell, many had not showered. We just couldn't relate to the scene so our whole group left right away." Another told me, "They sounded dogmatic and paranoid." "I just freaked and left," said another.

"It wasn't just race, it was also culture, although race was key."

In retrospect, observed Van Jones of STORM (Standing Together to Organize a Revolutionary Movement), "We should have stayed. We didn't see that we had a lot to learn from them. And they had a lot of materials for making banners, signs, puppets." "Later I went back and talked to people," recalled Rashidi, "and they were discussing tactics, very smart. Those folks were really ready for action. It was limiting for people of color to let that one experience affect their whole picture of white activists." Jinee Kim, a Korean American with the Third Eye Movement in the Bay Area, also thought it was a mistake. "We realized we didn't know how to do a blockade. We had no gas masks. They made sure everybody had food and water, they took care of people. We could have learned from them."

Reflecting the more positive evaluation of white protesters in general, Richard Moore, coordinator of the Southwest Network for Environmental and Economic Justice, told me "the white activists were very disciplined." "We sat down with whites, we didn't take the attitude that 'we can't work with white folks,' " concluded Rashidi. "It was a liberating experience."

Few predominantly white groups in the Bay Area made a serious effort to get people of color to Seattle. Juliette Beck of Global Exchange worked hard with others to help people from developing (third world) countries to come. For U.S. people of color, the main organizations that made a serious effort to do so were Just Act (Youth ACTion for Global JUSTice), formerly the Overseas Development Network, and Art and Revolution, which mostly helped artists. Many activists of color have mentioned Alli Starr of Art and Revolution, who not only helped people come out for the big march in Seattle, but also obtained a van with a sound system that was used by musicians and rappers.

In Just Act, Coumba Toure and two other members of color— Raj Jayadev and Malachi Larabee—pushed hard for support from the group. As a result, about 40 people of color were enabled to go thanks to special fundraising and whites staying at people's homes in Seattle so their hotel money could be used instead for plane tickets for people of color. Reflecting on the whole issue of working with whites, Coumba talked not only about pushing Just Act but also pushing people of color to apply for the help that became available.

One of the problems Coumba said she encountered in doing this was:

> "... a legacy of distrust of middle-class white activists that has emerged from experiences of 'being used.' Or not having our issues taken seriously. Involving people of color must be done in a way that gives them real space. Whites must understand a whole new approach is needed that includes respect (if you go to people of color thinking you know more, it creates a barrier). Also, you cannot approach people simply in terms of numbers, like 'let's give 2 scholarships.' People of color must be central to the project."

Jia Ching Chen recalled that once during the week of protest, in a jail holding cell, he was one of only two people of color among many Anglos. He discussed with some of them the need to involve more activists of color and the importance of white support in this. "Some would say, 'We want to diversify,' but didn't understand the dynamics of this." In other words, they didn't understand the kinds of problems described by Coumba Toure. "Other personal conversations were more productive," he said, "and some white people started to recognize why people of color could view the process of developing working relations with whites as oppressive."

Unfortunately the heritage of distrust was intensified by some of the AFL-CIO leadership on the November 30 march. They chose to take a different route through downtown rather than marching with others to the Convention Center and helping to block the WTO.

Yet if only a small number of people of color went to Seattle, all those with whom I spoke found the experience extraordinary. They spoke of being changed forever. "I saw the future." "I saw the possibility of people working together." They called the giant mobilization "a shot in the arm," if you had been feeling stagnant. "Being there was an incredible awakening." Naomi, a Filipina dancer and musician, recalled how "at first a lot of my group were tired, grumpy, wanting to go home. That really changed. One of the artists with us, who never considered herself a political activist, now wants to get involved back in Oakland. Seattle created a lot of strong bonds in my small community of coworkers and friends."

They seem to feel they had seen why, as the chant popularized by the Chicano/a students of MEChA goes, "Ain't no power like the power of the people, 'Cause the power of the people don't stop!"

There must be effective follow-up and increased communication between people of color across the nation: grassroots organizers, activists, cultural workers, and educators. We need to build on the contacts made (or that need to be made) from Seattle.

The opportunity to build on the WTO victory shines brightly. More than ever, we need to work on our ignorance about global issues with study groups, youth workshops, conferences. We need to draw specific links between the WTO and our close-to-home struggles in communities of color, as has been emphasized by Raj Jayadev and Lisa Juachon in *The Silicon Valley Reader: Localizing the Effects of the Global Economy*.

Many examples of how WTO has hurt poor people in third world countries were given during the protest. For example, a Filipino reported on indigenous farmers being compelled to use fertilizers containing poisonous chemicals in order to compete with cheap, imported potatoes. Ruined, they often left the land seeking survival elsewhere.

But there are many powerful examples right here in the U.S. For starters, consider:

* WTO policies encourage sub-livable wages for youth of color everywhere including right here.

* WTO policies encourage privatization of health care, education, welfare, and other crucial public services, as well as cut-

backs in government-provided services, so private industry can take them over and run them at a profit. This, along with sub-livable wages, leads to jeopardizing the lives of working-class people and criminalizing youth in particular.

* Workers in Silicon Valley are being chemically poisoned by the chips they work on that make great wealth for others. The WTO doesn't want to limit those profits with protection for workers.

* The WTO has said it is "unfair trade" to restrict the importation of gasoline which gives off high levels of cancer-causing chemicals. This could have a devastating effect on people in the U.S., including those of color, who buy that gas.

* Overall, the WTO is dominated by U.S. corporations. It is secretly run by a few advanced industrialized countries for the benefit of the rich and aspiring rich. The WTO serves to further impoverish the poor of all countries.

Armed with such knowledge, we can educate and organize people of color. As Jinee Kim said at a San Francisco report-back by youth of color, "We have to work with people who may not know the word 'globalization' but they live globalization."

We are confident in linking the conditions associated with current forms of debt relief, to our ongoing suffering. And we are committed to ending such conditions, replacing the Washington Consensus on neoliberal development with an African Consensus on genuine development, and adding to our demands the need for the reparations required to assure our society's ability to meet our basic human needs and to repair our basic human needs and to repair our degraded environments.

Lusaka Declaration, "Towards an African
Consensus on Sustainable Development
and Sustainable Solutions to the Debt
Crisis"
Lusaka, Zambia, May 19-21, 1999

10

Seattle and Beyond
Making the Connection
in the 21st Century

Manning Marable

It was immensely significant for black America that the last major public demonstration in the U.S. in the 20th century was a protest over global economics and trade. More than forty thousand people came to Seattle to oppose the policies of the World Trade Organization, which since 1995 has functioned like an international cabal in league with powerful corporate and financial interests. Labor activists went to Seattle to force the WTO to enact trade sanctions against nations that use child labor, prohibit labor unions and that pay slave wages to their workers. Environmental activists came to Seattle to pressure the WTO to ensure that environmental safeguards would be part of any global trade agreements.

What motivated both labor and environmentalists is the political recognition that issues like human rights, employment and healthcare cannot be addressed individually as separate issues. Nor can they be effectively discussed only in the context of a single nation-state. Capital is now truly global, and any analysis of specific socioeconomic problems that may exist in our country must be viewed from an international perspective.

The WTO was set up to be the global headquarters for drafting and enforcing trading rules. When one member country challenges another's trading practices, disputes are settled secretly by panels of trade experts. Elaine Bernard, director of Harvard's Trade Union Program, explains that the WTO's rules are based on privatization, free trade and few regulations on the environment. Bernard states the WTO's rules "value corporate power and commercial interests over labor and human rights, environmental and health concerns, and diversity. They increase inequality and stunt democracy. The WTO version of globalization is not a rising tide lifting all boats, as free traders insist, but a dangerous race to the bottom."

What kinds of "dangerous" priorities are we talking about? The WTO's rules deny Third World nations the right to have automatic licensing on patented but absolutely essential medicines. So, for example, even when African nations currently ravaged by diseases such as AIDS acquire the scientific and technical means to manufacture drugs to save millions of lives, the WTO's first concern is the protection of the patents and profits of powerful drug companies.

The WTO defines itself as a "trade" organization, which is incapable of pursuing social goals, such as extending the rights to freedom of collective bargaining to Third World and poor workers. Thus when an authoritarian regime markets clothing and athletic shoes that were produced by child labor under sweatshop conditions, the WTO claims that there is nothing it can do.

The demonstrations in Seattle, however, showed that growing numbers of Americans are recognizing that all of these issues—Third World sweatshops, the destruction of unions, deteriorating living standards, the dismantling of social programs inside the U.S.—are actually interconnected. "Globalization" is not some abstraction, but a destructive social force that has practical consequences on how we live, work and eat. There is a direct connection between the elimination of millions of jobs that can sustain families here in the U.S., and the exportation of jobs into countries without unions, environmental and safety standards. As real jobs disappear for millions of U.S. workers, and as welfare programs are eliminated, the only alternative is to use the prisons as the chief means of regulating mass unemployment.

Thus in the 1990s in the U.S., a period of so-called unprecedented capitalist expansion, the number of prisoners in federal, state and local correctional facilities roughly doubled. Between 1995 and 1997, according to the National Jobs for All Coalition, the average incomes of the poorest 20 percent of female-headed families fell. In 1998, 163 cities and 670 counties had unemployment rates that were more than 50 percent higher than the national average. These deep pockets of joblessness and hunger are not accidental: they represent the logical economic consequences of a nation that builds one hundred new prison cells a day and allows the export of millions of jobs.

Black Americans therefore should be in the forefront of the debates about international trade, but we must do so by recalling the activist slogan of the sixties: "Think Globally, Act Locally." There is an inescapable connection between Seattle and Sing Sing Prison, between global inequality and the brutalization of Third World labor and what's happening to black, brown and working people here in the United States.

As globalized capitalism destroys democracy, unions and the environment abroad, it is carrying out a similar agenda in our own backyards. For these reasons, we must create new organizations and a new political language that can unify international groups into collective protest action. We are challenged to build new political and information-sharing networks across the boundaries of race, gender, class and nation. We must make the connections in the fight for democracy in the 21st century.

11

Indigenous Peoples'
Seattle Declaration

Declaration by the Indigenous Peoples' Caucus convened and sponsored by the Indigenous Environmental Network, Seventh Generation Fund in alliance with the TEBTEBBA (Indigenous Peoples' Network for Policy Research and Education), International Indian Treaty Council, Indigenous Peoples Council on Biocolonialism and the Abya Yala Fund, on the occasion of the Third Ministerial Meeting of the World Trade Organization, November 30–December 3, 1999.

We, the Indigenous Peoples from various regions of the world, have come to Seattle to express our great concern over how the World Trade Organization is destroying Mother Earth and the cultural and biological diversity of which we are a part.

Trade liberalization and export-oriented development, which are the overriding principles and policies pushed by the WTO, are creating the most adverse impacts on the lives of Indigenous Peoples. Our inherent right to self-determination, our sovereignty as nations, and treaties and other constructive agreements which Indigenous nations and Peoples have negotiated with other nation-states, are undermined by most of the WTO Agreements. The disproportionate impact of these Agreements on our communities, whether through environmental degradation or the militarization and violence that often accompany development projects, is serious and must be addressed immediately.

The WTO Agreement on Agriculture (AOA), which promotes export competition and import liberalization, has allowed the entry of cheap agricultural products into our communities. It is causing the destruction of ecologically rational and sustainable agricultural practices of Indigenous Peoples.

Food security and the production of traditional food crops have been seriously compromised. Incidents of diabetes, cancers, and hypertension have significantly increased among Indigenous Peoples because of the scarcity of traditional foods and the dumping of junk food into our communities.

Small-scale farm production is giving way to commercial cash-crop plantations further concentrating ancestral lands into the hands of few agri-corporations and landlords. This has led to the dislocation of scores of people from our communities who then migrate to nearby cities and become the urban homeless and jobless.

The WTO Forests Products Agreement promotes free trade in forest products. By eliminating developed country tariffs on wood products by the year 2000, and developing country tariffs by 2003, the Agreement will result in the deforestation of many of the world's ecosystems in which Indigenous Peoples live.

Mining laws in many countries are being changed to allow free entry of foreign mining corporations, to enable them to buy and own mineral lands, and to freely displace Indigenous Peoples from their ancestral territories. These large-scale commercial mining and oil extraction activities continue to degrade our lands and fragile ecosystems, and pollute the soil, water, and air in our communities.

The appropriation of our lands and resources and the aggressive promotion of consumerist and individualistic Western culture continue to destroy traditional life-styles and cultures. The result is not only environmental degradation but also ill health, alienation, and high levels of stress manifested in high rates of alcoholism and suicide.

The theft and patenting of our biogenetic resources is facilitated by the TRIPs (Trade-Related Aspects of Intellectual Property Rights) of the WTO. Some plants which Indigenous Peoples have discovered, cultivated, and used for food, medicine, and for sacred rituals are already patented in the United States, Japan, and Europe. A few examples of these are *ayahuasca*, *quinoa*, and *sangre de drago* in forests of South America; kava in the Pacific; turmeric and bitter melon in Asia. Our access and control over our biological diversity and control over our traditional knowledge and intellectual heritage are threatened by the TRIPs Agreement.

Article 27.3b of the TRIPs Agreement allows the patenting of life-forms and makes an artificial distinction between plants, animals, and microorganisms. The distinction between "essentially biological" and "non-biological" and "microbiological" processes is also erroneous. As far as we are concerned all these are life-forms and life-creating processes which are sacred and which should not become the subject of private property ownership.

Finally, the liberalization of investments and the service sectors, which is pushed by the General Agreement on Trade in Services (GATS), reinforces the domination and monopoly control of foreign corporations over strategic parts of the economy.

The World Bank and the International Monetary Fund impose conditionalities of liberalization, deregulation and privatization on countries caught in the debt trap. These conditionalities are reinforced further by the WTO.

In light of the adverse impacts and consequences of the WTO Agreements identified above, we, Indigenous Peoples present the following demands:

We urgently call for a social and environmental justice analysis which will look into the Agreements' cumulative effects on Indigenous Peoples. Indigenous Peoples should be equal participants in establishing the criteria and indicators for these analyses so that they take into consideration spiritual as well as cultural aspects.

A review of the Agreements should be done to address all of the inequities and imbalances which adversely affect Indigenous Peoples. The proposals to address some of these are as follows:
1. For the Agreement on Agriculture

a. It should not include in its coverage small-scale farmers who are mainly engaged in production for domestic use and sale in local markets.

b. It should ensure the recognition and protection of rights of Indigenous Peoples to their territories and their resources, as well as their rights to continue practicing their indigenous sustainable agriculture and resource management practices and traditional livelihoods.

c. It should ensure the food security and the capacity of Indigenous Peoples to produce, consume and trade their traditional foods.

2. With regard to the liberalization of services and investments we recommend the following:

a. It must stop unsustainable mining, commercial planting of monocrops, dam construction, oil exploration, land conversion to golf clubs, logging, and other activities which destroy Indigenous Peoples' lands and violate the rights of Indigenous Peoples to their territories and resources.

b. The right of Indigenous Peoples to their traditional lifestyles, cultural norms and values should likewise be recognized and protected.

c. The liberalization of services, especially in the areas of health, should not be allowed if it will prevent Indigenous Peoples from having access to free, culturally appropriate as well as quality health services.

d. The liberalization of financial services, which makes the world a global casino, should be regulated.

3. On the TRIPs Agreement, our proposals are as follows:

a. Article 27.3b should be amended to categorically disallow the patenting of life-forms. It should clearly prohibit the patenting of microorganisms, plants, animals, including all their parts, whether they are genes, gene sequences, cells, cell lines, proteins or seeds.

b. It should also prohibit the patenting of natural processes, whether these are biological or microbiological, involving the use of plants, animals and microorganisms and their parts in producing variations of plants, animals and microorganisms.

c. It should ensure the exploration and development of alternative forms of protection outside of the dominant western intellectual property rights regime. Such alternatives must protect the knowledge and innovations and practices in agriculture, health care, and conservation of biodiversity, and should build upon indigenous methods and customary laws protecting knowledge, heritage and biological resources.

d. It should ensure that the protection offered to indigenous and traditional knowledge, innovation and practices is consistent with the Convention on Biological Diversity (i.e., Articles 8j, 10c, 17.2, and 18.4) and the International Undertaking on Plant Genetic Resources.

e. It should allow for the right of Indigenous Peoples and farmers to continue their traditional practices of saving, sharing and exchanging seeds, and cultivating, harvesting and using medicinal plants.

f. It should prohibit scientific researchers and corporations from appropriating and patenting indigenous seeds, medicinal plants, and related knowledge about these life-forms. The principles of prior informed consent and right of veto by Indigenous Peoples should be respected.

If the earlier proposals cannot be ensured, we call for the removal of the Agreement on Agriculture, the Forest Products Agreements and the TRIPs Agreement from the WTO.

We call on the member-states of the WTO not to allow another round while the review and rectification of the implementation of existing agreements has not been done. We reject the proposals for an investment treaty, competition, accelerated industrial tariffs, government procurement, and the creation of a working group on biotechnology.

We urge the WTO to reform itself to become democratic, transparent and accountable. If it fails to do this we call for the abolition of the WTO.

We urge the member nation-states of the WTO to endorse the adoption by the UN General Assembly of the current text of the UN Declaration on the Rights of Indigenous Peoples and the ratification of ILO Convention 169.

We call on the peoples' organizations and NGOs to support this "Indigenous Peoples' Seattle Declaration" and to promote it among their members.

We believe that the whole philosophy underpinning the WTO Agreements and the principles and policies it promotes contradict our core values, spirituality and worldviews, as well as our concepts and practices of development, trade and environmental protection. Therefore, we challenge the WTO to redefine its principles and practices toward a "sustainable communities" paradigm, and to recognize and allow for the continuation of other worldviews and models of development.

Indigenous Peoples, undoubtedly, are the ones most adversely affected by globalization and by the WTO Agreements. And it is we who can offer viable alternatives to the dominant economic growth, export-oriented development model. Our sustainable lifestyles and cultures, traditional knowledge, cosmologies, spirituality, values of collectivity, reciprocity, respect and reverence for Mother Earth are crucial in the search for a transformed society where justice, equity, and sustainability will prevail.

Indigenous Peoples' Organizations participating in the Seattle WTO protest that signed this Declaration are listed below:
- *Nilo Cayuquero*, Abya Yala Fund, U.S.A.
- *Victoria Tauli-Corpuz*, Indigenous Peoples Network for Policy Research and Education, Philippines
- *Tom Goldtooth*, Indigenous Environmental Network, U.S.A./Canada

- *Antonio Gonzales*, International Indian Treaty Council, International
- *Margarita Gutierrez*, Social Commission for The Development of the Nanhu, Mexico
- *Debra Harry*, Indigenous Peoples' Council on Biocolonialism, U.S.A.
- *Clemencia Herrera Nemarayema*, National Indigena Organization of Colombia, South America
- *Chief Johnny Jackson*, Klickitat Band of Yakama, Elder Committee of Indigenous Environmental Network, U.S.A./Canada
- *Carol Kalafatic*, International Indian Treaty Council, International
- *Dune Lankard*, Eyak Alaska Preservation Council, U.S.A.
- *Chief Arthur Manual*, Interior Alliance of First Nations, Canada
- *Alvin Manitopyes*, Cree Strong Heart Environmental and Wellness Society, Canada
- *Jim Main, Sr.*, Gros Ventre White Clay Society, U.S.A.
- *Jose Matos*, Indigenous Alliance Without Borders, U.S.A./Mexico
- *Esther Nahgahnub*, Anishinabeg Treaty 1854 Committee, U.S.A.
- *Chris Peters*, Seventh Generation Fund, U.S.A.
- *Priscilla Settee*, Indigenous Women's Network, USA/Canada
- *Taita Stanley*, Movimiento de la Juventad Kuna, Panama
- *Chaz Wheelock*, Great Lakes Regional Indigenous Environmental Network, U.S.A./Canada
- *Clemente Ibe Wilson*, Movimiento de la Juventad Kuna, Panama

Other Indigenous Peoples' Organizations, NGOs and individuals who wish to sign on to this statement should send email to ien@igc.org or tebtebba@skyinet.net.

12

Unity Statement of Philippine Social Movements, Labor Groups, Peoples' Organizations and NGOs

The Seattle events are a confluence of two politically significant factors: the massive and popular street protests that denounced the WTO and the whole "free trade" dogma; and the disunities and contradictions within the WTO itself that eventually led to the collapse of the trade talks. In both counts, i.e. both inside and outside the WTO convention hall, the U.S. failed to bully its way through.

Outside the convention hall, the U.S. government and western media had difficulty downplaying the massive street protests. They blamed the monstrous street riots to the handiwork of a few anarchists without saying that on the first day of the WTO meeting, dockworkers and cabdrivers in Seattle were on strike, residents were pouring into the streets offering food and water to the embattled protesters. Demonstrators in Seattle swelled to 70,000 while simultaneous rallies ranging from 50,000 to 70,000 were also happening in Paris, London, Geneva, India and other parts of the globe.

The "battle in Seattle" may not have directly caused the collapse of the trade talks but its political value lies in having stirred public consciousness on the evils of "free trade" and the WTO, which the general public previously thought to be a benign trade body. It serves to inspire a resurgence of people's struggles worldwide even if Seattle was only a spontaneous convergence of diverse political initiatives. If there is one lesson to be learned from the Seattle street protests, it was the significance of diverse ideological groups coming together in a common trajectory of rejecting the WTO and exposing all its evils.

Inside the convention hall, developing nations were one in blaming the WTO trade regime of delivering more benefits to the developed nations than to developing and least-developed nations. Such collective dismay was to be fired up later by the U.S. high-handed approach in introducing labor and environment issues into the domain of the WTO which developing nations view as a protectionist ploy intended to discriminate against third world exports. Aside from disagreement on many issues, developing nations decried the lack of transparency in the meeting where substantive talks are taking place through "green–room" negotiations without the knowledge and participation of most members. The big players on the other hand (like the U.S., EU and Japan) were outdoing each other in protecting their own economies over agricultural subsidies and anti-dumping laws and eventually competing over who gets the bigger pie in a "globalized" economic order. Such contradiction among competing monopoly powers also contributed to the breakdown of the talks.

Western media alleged that we, after having exulted in the success of frustrating the millennium round, were later sulking with the fact that labor and environment failed to be introduced into the WTO. This is completely misleading. As far as we in the social movements, labor and environmental groups are concerned, we have always upheld the promotion of labor rights and welfare and protection of the environment as key issues in our advocacy against "globalization." The logic of global corporate rule is to keep wages and labor standards low in developing countries to facilitate capital mobility and realize maximum profits from cheap and docile labor. It is also in developing countries where global capital engages in extractive industries to supply cheap raw materials, causing irreversible destruction to the environment and natural resource base of the third world. Clinton's agenda on these issues is hypocritical and a double-bladed weapon intended to give the WTO extra powers in micro-managing the economies of third world nations in addition to what the IMF and the World Bank have already been doing.

The collapse of the 3rd WTO ministerial meeting is therefore more than a matter of Clinton being ill-prepared with his agenda nor a case of the Seattle mayor's mishandling of the street protests. More than anything else, the WTO fiasco brought out the internal contradictions within the multilateral trading system and current crisis of the global capitalist system: a contradiction of global corporate rule versus the workers and the masses of oppressed peoples; of global capital represented by governments of developed nations versus developing and least-developed nations; and a contradiction among competing global economic powers.

Trade has been one major battleground so that global capital can conquer markets elsewhere while being able to protect their own home markets. For this purpose, the WTO was created using "free trade" as a pretext to pry open the economies of the third world in accordance with the dogma of "globalization" where supposedly no country can exist outside a "globalized" world economy.

The WTO fiasco proved the bankruptcy of the "free trade" and "globalization" ideology. The magnitude of people's protests and the shaping up of collective resistance by third world nations signaled a renewed challenge to the dominance of global capital.

The battle in Seattle won political gains for the people's struggle against the WTO and global capital but the war is far from over. The WTO is still in place and will resume talks on key areas like agriculture, services and intellectual property rights. We should not let our guards down and should vigorously oppose all attempts by the U.S. government to introduce new powers to the WTO. We must support the call of peasant movements worldwide to get agriculture out of the WTO even as we find ways of diminishing the hold of the WTO on such key areas of the economy. We should reject further liberalization of third world economies and work for a united front of all developing and least-developed nations in fighting for their national economic sovereignty and genuine development.

In the Philippines, we must continue to resist the Estrada government's plans of foolishly dragging the economy further under the control of foreign capital. Our campaign against charter change is a campaign for national sovereignty that should be pursued more resolutely. In the face of the WTO fiasco, we must urge the Estrada government to align itself with the growing anti-WTO sentiment of developing nations. It must review its negotiating position in the WTO and reverse previous commitments that have proven to be detrimental to workers, farmers, local producers and the whole economy. A legislative inquiry and review of the country's fate under the WTO must be supported.

"Shut down the WTO!" was the battle cry in Seattle that reverberated in all parts of the globe. We, in the Philippine social movements, labor organizations, peasant associations, NGOs and other people's organizations are committed to pursue this battle cry in solidarity with other oppressed peoples and nations of the world.

Signed:
- *Eduardo Mora*, Pambansang Katipunan ng Makabayang Magbubukid (PKMM, National Assoc. of Patriotic Peasants)
- *Sonia Soto*, Kilusan para sa Pambansang Demokrasya (KPD, Movement for Nationalism and Democracy)
- *Cris Gaerlan*, ALAB KATIPUNAN
- *Prof. Walden Bello*, AKBAYAN
- *Joel Rodriguez*, Management and Organizational Development for Empowerment (MODE)
- *Lidy Nacpil*, Freedom from Debt Coalition (FDC)
- *Sonny Melencio*, Sosyalistang Partido ng Paggawa (SPP, Socialist Party of Labor)
- *Arze Glipo*, Integrated Rural Development Foundation (IRDF)
- *Primo Amparo*, Manggagawa para sa Kalayaan ng Bayan (MAKABAYAN, Workers for Social Liberation)
- *Jaime Regalario*, KATAPAT (Movement for National Patronage)

- *Eric Guitterrez*, Institute for Popular Democracy (IPD)
- *Fr. Albert Suatengco*, Philippine-Asia Jubilee Campaign Against the Debt (PAJCAD)
- *Alice Raymundo*, PKMM—Women's Committee
- *Susan Granada*, Philippine Jubilee Network (PJN)
- *Sr. ArnoldMaria Noel*, Association of Local Women Religious of the Archdiocese of Manila
- *Naty Bernardino*, International South Group Network—Manila (ISGN)
- *Francisco Pascual*, Resource Center for People's Development (RCPD)

Since most of the Middle East governments lack democratic legitimacy, and to various degrees are dependent on external forces to prop them up, they are unlikely to resist the IMF model and embrace an alternative development agenda without significant pressure from below and greater democratization across the region. But the opening created by the protests in Seattle and the growing grassroots mobilization around the world against trade and investment deregulation, particularly in the developing world, may help encourage such democratic efforts in the Middle East.

Ghassan Bishara,
Middle East Research and
Information Project

Section Three

The Case Against the WTO

The many groups that assembled in the streets of Seattle were equipped with a detailed critique that had been developed through publications, teach-ins and other forms of grassroots education. This section of the book presents just some of the ammunition the movement has compiled arguing for the abolition of the WTO.

In "Top Ten Reasons to Oppose the WTO," Juliette Beck and Kevin Danaher provide a concise, popular critique explaining why the WTO is beyond repair.

Walden Bello's essay, "Reforming the WTO is the Wrong Agenda," displays his usual erudition in showing that the WTO was created by a fundamentally undemocratic process and is not capable of giving fair treatment to the former colonial countries.

Vandana Shiva, in "Spinning a New Mythology," takes apart the WTO's new claim that it is concerned with poverty.

In "Will a Social Clause in Trade Agreements Advance International Solidarity?" David Bacon takes on the mainstream trade union position that the WTO can effectively be reformed by adding amendments for protecting the rights of workers.

The Environmental Research Foundation, shows that the WTO "Turns Back the Environmental Clock" on how humanity governs its natural resources.

Peter Rosset concludes the section by outlining how "A New Food Movement" came of age at the WTO protests in Seattle.

13

Top Ten Reasons to Oppose the World Trade Organization

Juliette Beck and Kevin Danaher

1. The WTO advances corporate-managed trade at all costs.

The WTO is not a democratic institution, yet its policies impact all aspects of society and the planet. WTO rules are essentially written by corporations who have inside access to the negotiations. For example, the U.S. Trade Representative relies on its 17 "Industry Sector Advisory Committees" for input on trade talks. These committees are made up of business representatives. Citizen input by consumer, environmental, human rights and labor organizations is ignored and requests for information are denied. Even worse, the Clinton-Gore Administration has chosen to appeal a recent court decision requiring environmental representatives on two advisory committees that deal with forest issues.

2. The WTO is a stacked, secretive court.

The WTO's dispute panels rule on whether or not a nation's laws are "barriers to trade" behind closed doors with no public input allowed. The panels are comprised of three trade bureaucrats who are not screened for conflict of interest. For example, in the tuna/dolphin case that Mexico filed against the U.S. (which forced the U.S. to repeal its law barring tuna caught by purse-seine nets that needlessly kill hundreds of thousands of dolphins per year), one of the judges was from a corporate front group that lobbied on behalf of the Mexican government for NAFTA. In all its cases to date involving laws protecting public health and the environment, the WTO has ruled in favor of corporations.

3. The WTO tramples over labor and human rights.

WTO agreements forbid the regulation of a product based on the way it is produced, regardless if the product was made with child labor or by workers exposed to toxic chemicals. A Government Accounting Office study found that the U.S. law banning products made with forced labor violates WTO rules. Furthermore, governments are not allowed to take human rights into consideration when deciding how tax dollars should be spent; purchasing decisions can only be based on commercial considerations such as quality and cost. The Massachusetts law against contracting with corporations that do business with the brutal military dictatorship of Burma is currently being challenged in the WTO. International labor issues are relegated to the International Labor Organization, which unlike the WTO has no enforcement capacity. The ILO has found Burma in violation of key labor standards, but Burma is still considered an equal member of the WTO.

4. WTO policies are widening the gap between the rich and poor.

The UN Development Program's *Human Development Report* for 1999 states: "The top fifth of the world's people in the richest countries enjoy 82% of the expanding export trade and 68% of foreign direct investment, while the bottom fifth get barely more than 1 percent. These trends reinforce economic stagnation and low human development." In the U.S., a pro-free trade economist has determined that 39 percent of the increase in income inequality can be attributed to trade. Studies have shown that employers often use the threat of relocation to low wage countries in order to ratchet down wages and benefits.

5. The WTO is anti-environment.

The WTO is being used by corporations to dismantle hard-won environmental protections. In 1993, the very first WTO panel ruled against a regulation of the U.S. Clean Air Act, which had required both domestic and foreign producers alike to produce cleaner gasoline. Recently, the WTO declared illegal the provision of the Endangered Species Act that requires shrimp sold in the U.S. to be caught with an inexpensive 'turtle-excluder device' that allows endangered sea turtles to escape shrimp nets. The WTO ruled against the law, calling it an illegal encroachment on the sovereignty of other governments for the U.S. to set rules for what can be sold in the United States.

6. The WTO rules undermine public health.

The WTO's fierce defense of intellectual property rights (patents, copyrights and trademarks) comes at the expense of health and human lives. The WTO's support of pharmaceutical companies against governments seeking to protect people's health has serious implications for places like sub-Saharan Africa, where 80 percent of the world's new AIDS cases are found. In the WTO ruling against the European Union's ban on beef grown with hormones, the WTO completely disregarded the common sense notion that chemical additives should be proven safe before they are used ("precautionary principle").

7. The WTO was undemocratically established.

During the U.S. Congressional debate in 1994, Public Citizen offered a $10,000 donation to the charity of choice of any Congressperson who had read the entire GATT/WTO legislation. Colorado Republican Hank Brown accepted the challenge. Although he originally planned to vote in favor of GATT, after reading the text, he was appalled and could not support it. The WTO implementing legislation made many changes to U.S. laws that most lawmakers were unaware of. Had the agreement been voted on as a treaty, requiring a two-thirds Senate majority, it would have been defeated.

8. The WTO is undemocratic and unaccountable.

The WTO claims that it operates by consensus, but the Seattle debacle illustrates how the WTO really functions. After much of the ministerial declaration was drafted in private "green room" meetings with select countries present, African and Caribbean countries effectively banded together for the first time. They denounced the closed-door process and blocked the launching of a new round. The WTO boasts of its interference with the democratic process within countries as well. Their website states: "Under WTO rules, once a commitment has been made to liberalize a sector of trade, it is difficult to reverse... Quite often, governments use the WTO as a welcome external constraint on their policies: 'we can't do this because it would violate the WTO agreements.'"

9. The WTO hurts countries in the Global South.

Leaders of the global South are developing a newconsensus that free trade policies result in great wealth for a few, and impoverishment of the many. Under WTO rules, developing countries are prohibited from following the same polices that industrialized countries pursued, such as protecting young, domestic industries until they can be internationally competitive. Local policies aimed at rewarding countries that hire a certain percentage of local residents, transfer technology and use domestic inputs are essentially illegal under the WTO.

10. The tide is turning against free trade and the WTO!

There is a growing international backlash against the WTO and the corporate globalization over which it presides. Movement-building by coalitions such as People's Global Action, the Direct Action Network, the Citizen's Trade Campaign, the Fifty Years Is Enough Network, and the Alliance for Sustainable Jobs & the Environment are growing fast, as public support for a corporate-managed global economy dwindles. A January 2000 opinion poll by *Business Week* found that 52 percent of Americans sympathized with us protestors at the WTO in Seattle.

In sum, the WTO was created to serve corporate interests and should be dismantled before it causes more harm to workers, the environment and democracy itself.

Those castigating China and other developing countries need to recognize that the U.S. use of trade sanctions to punish countries that violate human rights is hypocritical. They forget the fact that the U.S. itself has yet to ratify the International Covenant for Economic, Social and Cultural Rights (ICESCR), the Convention on the Rights of the Child as well as the Convention on All Forms of Discrimination Against Women (CEDAW). It is not coincidental that the only industrialized country to reject basic human rights also boasts the highest disparity between the rich and poor, and the highest child poverty rates, with one in five children growing up in poverty. And yet, it assumes moral authority when it comes to human rights.

Anyone who is opposed to the Chinese joining the WTO or being granted the most-favored nation status based on its human rights record needs to be reminded that the USA has, in many instances, acted like the rogue nations it criticizes. Since when has the U.S economic system become the paragon of virtue? Maybe other WTO members should be offended by the quasi-slavery conditions faced by farm workers in parts of the U.S., or by prison labor and sweatshops in America. Any member country could say that U.S. law, which makes it possible to execute a teenager, is an offense against humanity. These and other charges might form the justification for an embargo on U.S. exports or for its expulsion from the WTO!

Anuradha Mittal, Food First

14

Reforming the WTO
Is the Wrong Agenda

Walden Bello

In the wake of the collapse of the Seattle Ministerial, there
has emerged the opinion that reform of the WTO is now
the program that NGOs, governments, and citizens must
embrace. The collapse of the WTO Ministerial is said to provide
a unique window of opportunity for a reform agenda.

Cited by some as a positive sign is United States Trade Representative Charlene Barshefsky's comment, immediately after
the collapse of the Seattle Ministerial, that:

...the WTO has outgrown the processes appropriate to an
earlier time. An increasing and necessary view, generally
shared among the members, was that we needed a process
which had a greater degree of internal transparency and
inclusion to accommodate a larger and more diverse membership.[1]

Also seen as an encouraging gesture is UK Secretary of State
for Trade and Industry Stephen Byers' recent statement to Com-
monwealth Trade Ministers in New Delhi that the "WTO will
not be able to continue in its present form. There has to be fundamental and radical change in order for it to meet the needs and
aspirations of all 134 of its members."[2]

These are, in our view, damage control statements and provide little indication of the seriousness about reform of the two governments that were, pre-Seattle, the stoutest defenders of the inequalities built into the structure, dynamics, and objectives of the WTO. It is unfortunate that they are now being cited to convince developing countries and NGOs to take up an agenda of reform that could lead precisely to the strengthening of an organization that is very fundamentally flawed.

What civil society, North and South, should instead be doing at this point is radically cutting down the power of the institution and reducing it to simply another institution in a pluralistic world trading system with multiple systems of governance.

Does World Trade Need the World Trade Organization?

This is the fundamental question on which the question of reform hinges. World trade did not need the WTO to expand 87-fold between 1948 and 1997, from $124 billion to $10,772 billion.[3] This expansion took place under the flexible GATT trade regime. The WTO's founding in 1995 did not respond to a collapse or crisis of world trade such as happened in the 1930s. It was not necessary for global peace, since no world war or trade-related war had taken place during that period. In the seven major inter-state wars that took place in that period—the Korean War of 1950–53, the Vietnam War of 1945–75, the Suez Crisis of 1956, the 1967 Arab-Israeli War, the 1973 Arab-Israeli War, the 1982 Falklands War, and the Gulf War of 1990—trade conflict did not figure even remotely as a cause.

GATT was, in fact, functioning reasonably well as a framework for liberalizing world trade. Its dispute-settlement system was flexible and with its recognition of the "special and differential status" of developing countries, it provided the space in a global economy for Third World countries to use trade policy for development and industrialization.

Why was the WTO established following the Uruguay Round of 1986–94? Of the major trading powers, Japan was very ambivalent, concerned as it was to protect its agriculture as well as its particular system of industrial production that, through formal and informal mechanisms, gave its local producers primary right to exploit the domestic market. The EU, well on the way to becoming a self-sufficient trading bloc, was likewise ambivalent, knowing that its highly subsidized system in agriculture would come under attack. Though demanding greater access to their manufactured and agricultural products in the Northern economies, the developing countries did not see this as being accomplished through a comprehensive agreement enforced by a powerful trade bureaucracy but through discrete negotiations and agreements in the model of the Integrated Program for Commodities (IPCs) and Commodity Stabilization Fund agreed upon under the aegis of UNCTAD in the late seventies.

The founding of the WTO primarily served the interest of the United States. Just as it was the U.S. which blocked the founding of the International Trade Organization (ITO) in 1948, when it felt that this would not serve its position of overwhelming economic dominance in the postwar world, so it was the U.S. that became the dominant lobbyist for the comprehensive Uruguay Round and the founding of the WTO in late eighties and early nineties, when it felt that more competitive global conditions had created a situation where its corporate interests now demanded an opposite stance.

Just as it was Washington's threat in the 1950s to leave GATT if the U.S. was not allowed to maintain protective mechanisms for milk and other agricultural products that led to agricultural trade's exemption from GATT rules, so was it U.S. pressure that brought agriculture into the GATT-WTO system in 1995. And the reason for Washington's change of mind was articulated quite candidly by then U.S. Agriculture Secretary John Block at the start of the Uruguay Round negotiations in 1986: "[The] idea that developing countries should feed themselves is an anachronism from a bygone era. They could better ensure their food security by relying on U.S. agricultural products, which are available, in most cases at much lower cost."[4] Washington, of course, did not have only developing country markets in mind, but also Japan, South Korea, and the European Union.

It was mainly the U.S. that pushed to bring services under WTO coverage, with its assessment that in the new burgeoning area of international services, and particularly in financial services, its corporations had a lead that needed to be preserved. It was also the U.S. that pushed to expand WTO jurisdiction to the so-called "Trade-Related Investment Measures" (TRIMs) and "Trade-Related Intellectual Property Rights" (TRIPs). The first sought to eliminate barriers to the system of internal cross-border trade of product components among TNC (transnational corporation) subsidiaries that had been imposed by developing countries in order to develop their industries; the second to consolidate the U.S. advantage in the cutting-edge knowledge-intensive industries.

And it was the U.S. that forced the creation of the WTO's formidable dispute-resolution and enforcement mechanism after being frustrated with what U.S. trade officials considered weak GATT efforts to enforce rulings favorable to the United States. As Washington's academic point man on trade, C. Fred Bergsten, head of the Institute of International Economics, told the U.S. Senate, the strong WTO dispute settlement mechanism serves U.S. interests because "we can now use the full weight of the international machinery to go after those trade barriers, reduce them, get them eliminated."[5]

In sum, it has been Washington's changing perception of the needs of its economic interest groups that have shaped and re-shaped the international trading regime. It was not global necessity that gave birth to the WTO in 1995. It was the U.S.'s assessment that the interests of its corporations were no longer served by a loose and flexible GATT but needed an all-powerful and wide-ranging WTO. From the free-market paradigm that underpins it, to the rules and regulations set forth in the different agreements that make up the Uruguay Round, to its system of decision-making and accountability, the WTO is a blueprint for the global hegemony of Corporate America. It seeks to institutionalize the accumulated advantages of U.S. corporations.

Is the WTO necessary? Yes, to the United States. But not to

the rest of the world. The necessity of the WTO is one of the biggest lies of our time, and its acceptance is due to the same propaganda principle practiced by Joseph Goebbels: if you repeat a lie often enough, it will be taken as truth.

Can the WTO Serve the Interests of Developing Countries?

Is the WTO a necessary structure—one that, whatever its flaws, brings more benefits than costs, and would therefore merit efforts at reform? When the Uruguay Round was being negotiated, there was considerable lack of enthusiasm for the process by the developing countries. After all, these countries had formed the backbone of UNCTAD (United Nations Conference on Trade and Development), which, with its system of one-country/one-vote and majority voting, they felt was an international arena more congenial to their interests. They entered the Uruguay Round greatly resenting the large trading powers' policy of weakening and marginalizing UNCTAD in the late seventies and early eighties. Largely passive spectators, with a great number not even represented during the negotiations owing to resource constraints, the developing countries were dragged into unenthusiastic endorsement of the Marrakesh Accord of 1994 that sealed the Uruguay Round and established the WTO. True, there were some developing countries, most of them in the Cairns Group of developed and developing country agro-exporters, that actively promoted the WTO in the hope that they would gain greater market access for their exports, but they were a small minority.

To sell the WTO to the South, U.S. propagandists evoked the fear that staying out of the WTO would result in a country's isolation from world trade ("like North Korea") and stoked the promise that a "rules-based system" of world trade would protect the weak countries from unilateral acts by the big trading powers.

By 1994 the developing countries were in a weakened position. With their economies dominated by the IMF and the World Bank; with the structural adjustment programs pushed by these agencies focusing on radical trade liberalization; and being much weaker as a bloc owing to the debt crisis of the 1980s, as compared to the 1970s and the height of the "New International Economic Order," most developing country delegations felt they had no choice but to sign on the dotted line.

Over the next few years, however, these countries realized that they had signed away their right to employ a variety of critical trade measures for development purposes.

In contrast to the loose GATT framework, which had allowed some space for development initiatives, the comprehensive and tightened Uruguay Round was fundamentally anti-development in its thrust.

Loss of Trade Policy as a Development Tool

In signing on to GATT, Third World countries were committed to banning all quantitative restrictions on imports, reducing tariffs on many industrial imports, and promising not to raise tariffs on all other imports. In so doing, they effectively gave up the use of trade policy to pursue industrialization objectives. The way that the NICs, or "newly industrializing countries," made it to industrial status, via the policy of import substitution, is now effectively removed as a route to industrialization.

The anti-industrialization thrust of the GATT-WTO Accord is made even more manifest in the Agreement on Trade-Related Investment Measures (TRIMs) and the Agreement on Trade-Related Intellectual Property Rights (TRIPs). In their drive to industrialize, NICs like South Korea and Malaysia made use of many innovative mechanisms such as trade-balancing requirements that tied the value of a foreign investor's imports of raw materials and components to the value of their exports of the finished commodity, or "local content" regulations which mandated that a certain percentage of the components that went into the making of a product was sourced locally.

These rules indeed restricted the maneuvering space of foreign investors, but they were successfully employed by the NICs to marry foreign investment to national industrialization. They enabled the NICs to raise income from capital-intensive exports, develop support industries, bring in technology, while still protecting local entrepreneurs' preferential access to the domestic market. In Malaysia, for instance, the strategic use of local content policy enabled the Malaysians to build a "national car," in cooperation with Mitsubishi, that has now achieved about 80 per cent local content and controls 70 per cent of the Malaysian market. Thanks to the TRIMs accord, these mechanisms are now illegal.

The Restriction of Technological Diffusion

Like the TRIMs agreement, the TRIPs regime is seen as effectively opposed to the industrialization and development efforts of Third World countries. This becomes clear from a survey of the economic history not only of the NICs but of almost all late-industrializing countries. A key factor in their industrial take-off was their relatively easy access to cutting-edge technology: The U.S. industrialized, to a great extent by using but paying very little for British manufacturing innovations, as did the Germans. Japan industrialized by liberally borrowing U.S. technological innovations, but barely compensating the Americans for this. And the Koreans industrialized by copying quite liberally (with little payment) U.S. and Japanese product and process technologies.

But what is "technological diffusion" from the perspective of the late industrializer is "piracy" from that of the industrial leader. The TRIPs regime takes the side of the latter and makes the process of industrialization by imitation much more difficult from here on. It represents what UNCTAD describes as "a premature strengthening of the intellectual property system ... that favors monopolistically controlled innovation over broad-based diffusion."[6]

The TRIPs regime provides a generalized minimum patent protection of 20 years; increases the duration of the protection for semiconductors or computer chips; institutes draconian border regulations against products judged to be violating intellectual property rights; and places the burden of proof on the presumed violator of process patents.

The TRIPs accord is a victory for the U.S. high-tech industry, which has long been lobbying for stronger controls over the diffusion of innovations. Innovation in the knowledge-intensive high-tech sector—in electronic software and hardware, biotechnology, lasers, opto-electronics, liquid crystal technology, to name a few—has become the central determinant of economic power in our time. And when any company in the NICs and Third World wishes to innovate, say in chip design, software programming, or computer assembly, it necessarily has to integrate several patented designs and processes, most of them from U.S. electronic hardware and software giants like Microsoft, Intel and Texas Instruments.[7] As the Koreans have bitterly learned, exorbitant multiple royalty payments to what has been called the American "high-tech mafia" keeps one's profit margins very low while reducing incentives for local innovation.

The likely outcome is for a Southern manufacturer simply to pay royalties for a technology rather than to innovate, thus perpetuating the technological dependence on Northern firms. Thus, TRIPs enables the technological leader, in this case the United States, to greatly influence the pace of technological and industrial development in rival industrialized countries, the NICs, and the Third World.

Diluting the "Special and Differential Treatment" Principle
The central principle of UNCTAD—an organization disempowered by the establishment of the WTO—is that owing to the critical nexus between trade and development, developing countries must not be subjected to the same expectations, rules, and regulations that govern trade among the developed countries. Owing to historical and structural considerations, developing countries need special consideration and special assistance in leveling the playing field for them to be able to participate equitably in world trade. This would include both the use of protective tariffs for development purposes and preferential access of developing country exports to developed country markets.

While GATT was not centrally concerned with development,

it did recognize the special status of the developing countries, requiring "Special and Differential Treatment" (SDT). Perhaps the strongest statement of this was in the Tokyo Round Declaration in 1973, which recognized "the importance of the application of differential measures in developing countries in ways which will provide special and more favorable treatment for them in areas of negotiation where this is feasible."[8] Different sections of the evolving GATT code allowed countries to renegotiate tariff bindings in order to promote the establishment of certain industries; allowed developing countries to use tariffs for economic development and fiscal purposes; allowed them to use quantitative restrictions to promote infant industries; and conceded the principle of non-reciprocity by developing countries in trade negotiation.[9] The 1979 Framework Agreement, known as the Enabling Clause, also provided a permanent legal basis for General System of Preferences (GSP) schemes that would provide preferential access for developing country exports.[10]

A significant shift occurred in the Uruguay Round. GSP schemes were not bound, meaning tariffs could be raised against developing countries until they equaled the bound rates applied to imports from all sources. Indeed, during the negotiations, the threat to remove GSP was used as "a form of bilateral pressure on developing countries."[11] SDT was turned from a focus on a special right to protect and special rights of market access to "one of responding to special adjustment difficulties in developing countries stemming from the implementation of WTO decisions."[12] Measures meant to address the structural inequality of the trading system gave way to measures, such as a lower rate of tariff reduction or a longer time frame for implementing decisions, which regarded the problem of developing countries as simply that of catching up in an essentially even playing field.

SDT has been watered down in the WTO, and this is not surprising because the neoliberal agenda that underpins the WTO philosophy differs from the Keynesian assumptions of GATT: that there are no special rights, no special protections needed for development. The only route to development is one that involves radical trade and investment liberalization.

Fate of the Special Measures for Developing Countries

Perhaps the best indicators of the marginal consideration given to developing countries in the WTO is the fate of the measures that were supposed to respond to the special conditions of developing countries. There were three key agreements which promoters of the WTO claimed were specifically designed to meet the needs of the South:

• The Special Ministerial Agreement approved in Marrakesh in April 1994, which decreed that special compensatory measures would be taken to counteract the negative effects of trade liberalization on the net food-importing developing countries;

• The Agreement on Textiles and Clothing, which mandated that the system of quotas on developing country exports of textiles and garments to the North would be dismantled over ten years;

• The Agreement on Agriculture, which, while "imperfect," nevertheless was said to promise greater market access to developing country agricultural products and begin the process of bringing down the high levels of state support and subsidization of EU and U.S. agriculture, which was resulting in the dumping of massive quantities of grain on Third World markets.

What happened to these measures?

The Special Ministerial Decision taken at Marrakesh to provide assistance to net food-importing countries to offset the reduction of subsidies that would make food imports more expensive for the net food-importing countries has never been implemented. Though world crude oil prices more than doubled in 1995/96, the World Bank and the IMF scotched an idea of any offsetting aid by arguing that "the price increase was not due to the Agreement on Agriculture, and besides there was never any agreement anyway on who would be responsible for providing the assistance."[13]

The Agreement on Textiles and Clothing committed the developed countries to bring under WTO discipline all textile and garment imports over four stages, ending on January 1, 2005. A key feature was supposed to be the lifting of quotas on imports restricted under the Multifiber Agreement (MFA) and similar schemes which had been used to contain penetration of developed country markets by cheap clothing and textile imports from the Third World. Yet developed countries retained the right to choose which product lines to liberalize when, so that they first brought mainly unrestricted products into the WTO discipline and postponed dealing with restricted products until much later. Thus, in the first phase, all restricted products continued to be under quota, as only items where imports were not considered threatening (such as felt hats or yarn of carded fine animal hair) were included in the developed countries' notifications. Indeed, the notifications for the coverage of products for liberalization on January 1, 1998 showed that "even at the second stage of implementation only a very small proportion" of restricted products would see their quotas lifted.[14]

Given this trend, John Whalley notes that "the belief is now widely held in the developing world that in 2004, while the MFA may disappear, it may well be replaced by a series of other trade instruments, possibly substantial increases in anti-dumping duties."[15]

The Agreement on Agriculture (AOA), was sold to developing countries during the Uruguay Round as a major step toward providing market access for developing country exports, and bringing down the high levels of domestic support for first-world farming interests that results in dumping of commodities in third world markets. Yet after five years, there have been few gains in market access into developed country markets, and this has been accompanied by even higher levels of overall subsidization of developed country exports through ingenious combinations of export subsidies, export credits, market support, and various kinds of direct income payments.

The figures speak for themselves: the level of overall subsidization of agriculture in the OECD countries rose from $182 billion in 1995 when the WTO was born to $280 billion in 1997 to $362 billion in 1998! Instead of the beginning of a New Deal, the AOA, in the words of a former Philippine Secretary of Trade, "has perpetuated the unevenness of a playing field which the multilateral trading system has been trying to correct. Moreover, this has placed the burden of adjustment on developing countries relative to countries who can afford to maintain high levels of domestic support and export subsidies."[16]

The collapse of the agricultural negotiations in Seattle is the best example of how extremely difficult it is to reform the AOA. The European Union opposed till the bitter end language in an agreement that would commit it to "significant reduction" of its subsidies. But the U.S. was not blameless. It resolutely opposed any effort to cut back on its forms of subsidies such as export credits, direct income for farmers, and "emergency" farm aid, as well as any mention of its practice of dumping products in developing country markets.

Oligarchic Decision-Making as a Central, Defining Process

Is the system of WTO decision-making reformable? While far more flexible than the WTO, the GATT was, of course, far from perfect, and one of the bad traits that the WTO took over from it was the system of decision-making. GATT functioned through a process called "consensus." This definition of consensus responded to the same problem that faced the IMF and the World Bank's developed country members: how to assure control at a time when the numbers gave the edge to the new countries of the South. In the Fund and the Bank, the system of decision-making had the weight of a country's vote determined by the size of its capital subscriptions, which gave the U.S. and the other rich countries effective control of the two organizations.

In the GATT, a one-country one-vote system was initially tried, but the big trading powers saw this as inimical to their interests. Thus, the last time a vote was taken in GATT was in 1959.[17] The system that finally emerged was described by U.S. economist Bergsten as one that "does not work by voting. It works by a consensus arrangement which, to tell the truth, is managed by four—the Quads: the United States, Japan, European Union, and Canada."[18] He continued: "Those countries have to agree if any major steps are going to be made, that is true. But no votes."[19]

Indeed, so undemocratic is the WTO that decisions are arrived at informally, via caucuses convoked in the corridors of the ministerial meetings by the big trading powers. The formal plenary sessions, which in democracies are the central arena for decision-making, are reserved for speeches. The key agreements to come out of the first and second ministerials of the WTO—the decision to liberalize information technology trade taken at the first ministerial in Singapore in 1996 and the agreement to liberalize trade in electronic commerce arrived at in Geneva in 1998—were all decided in informal backroom sessions and simply presented to the full assembly as *faits accompli*. Consensus simply functioned to render non-transparent a process where smaller, weaker countries were pressured, browbeaten, or bullied to conform to the "consensus" forged among major trading powers.

With surprising frankness, at a press conference in Seattle, U.S. Trade Representative Charlene Barshefsky, who played the pivotal role in all three ministerials, described the dynamics and consequences of this system of decision-making: "The process, including even at Singapore as recently as three years ago, was a rather exclusionary one. All meetings were held between 20 and 30 key countries ... And that meant 100 countries, 100, were never in the room ... [T]his led to an extraordinarily bad feeling that they were left out of the process and that the results even at Singapore had been dictated to them by the 25 or 30 privileged countries who were in the room."[20]

Then, after registering her frustration at the WTO delegates' failing to arrive at consensus via supposedly broader "working groups" set up for the Seattle ministerial, Barshefsky warned delegates: "...[I] have made very clear and I reiterated to all ministers today that, if we are unable to achieve that goal, I fully reserve the right to also use a more exclusive process to achieve a final outcome. There is no question about either my right as the chair to do it or my intention as the chair to do it...."[21]

And she was serious about ramming through a declaration at the expense of non-representativeness, with India, one of the key developing country members of the WTO, being "routinely excluded from private talks organized by the United States in last ditch efforts to come up with a face-saving deal."[22]

In damage-containment mode after the collapse of the Seattle Ministerial, Barshefsky, WTO Director-General Mike Moore, and other rich country representatives have spoken about the need for WTO "reform." But none have declared any intention of pushing for a one-county/one-vote majority decision-making system or a voting system weighted by population size, which would be the only fair and legitimate methods in a democratic international organization. The fact is, such mechanisms will never be adopted, for this would put the developing countries in a preponderant role in terms of decision-making.

Should One Try to Reform a Jurassic Institution?

Reform is a viable strategy when the system is question is fundamentally fair but has simply been corrupted such as the case with some democracies. It is not a viable strategy when a system is so fundamentally unequal in purposes, principles, and processes as the WTO. The WTO systematically protects the economic advantages of the rich countries, particularly the United States. It is based on a paradigm that denigrates the right to take activist measures to achieve development on the part of less developed countries, thus leading to a radical dilution of their right to "special and differential treatment." The WTO raises inequality into a principle of decision-making.

The WTO is often promoted as a "rules-based" trading framework that protects the weaker and poorer countries from unilateral actions by the stronger states. The opposite is true: the WTO, like many other multilateral international agreements, is meant to institutionalize and legitimize inequality. Its main purpose is to reduce the tremendous policing costs to the stronger powers that would be involved in disciplining many small countries in a more fluid, less structured international system. It is not surprising that both the WTO and the IMF are currently mired in a severe crisis of legitimacy. Both are highly centralized, highly unaccountable, highly non-transparent global institutions that seek to subjugate, control, or harness vast swathes of global economic, social, political, and environmental processes to the needs and interests of a global minority of states, elites and TNCs. The dynamics of such institutions clash with the burgeoning democratic aspirations of peoples, countries, and communities in both the North and the South. The centralizing dynamics of these institutions clash with the efforts of communities and nations to regain control of their fate and achieve a modicum of security by deconcentrating and decentralizing economic and political power. In other words, these are Jurassic institutions in an age of participatory political and economic democracy.

Building a Pluralistic System of Trade Governance

If there is one thing that is clear, it is that developing country governments and international civil society must not allow their energies to be hijacked into reforming these institutions. This would amount to giving a facelift to fundamentally flawed institutions. Indeed, today's need is not another centralized global institution, reformed or unreformed, but the deconcentration and decentralization of institutional power and the creation of a pluralistic system of institutions and organizations interacting with one another amid broadly defined and flexible agreements and understandings. It was under such a relatively pluralistic global system, where hegemonic power was still far from institutionalized in a set of all-encompassing and powerful multilateral organizations that the Latin American countries and many Asian countries were able to achieve a modicum of industrial development in the period from 1950–70. It was under a more pluralistic world system, under a GATT that was limited in its power, flexible, and more sympathetic to the special status of developing countries, that the East and Southeast Asian countries were able to become newly industrializing countries through activist state trade and industrial policies that departed significantly from the free-market biases enshrined in the WTO.

The alternative to a powerful WTO is not a Hobbesian state of nature. It is always the powerful that have stoked this fear. The reality of international economic relations in a world marked by a multiplicity of international and regional institutions that check one another is a far cry from the propaganda image of a "nasty" and "brutish" world. Of course, the threat of unilateral action by the powerful is ever present in such a system, but it is one that even the powerful hesitate to take for fear of its consequences on their legitimacy as well as the reaction it would provoke in the form of opposing coalitions.

In other words, what developing countries and international civil society should aim at is not to reform the WTO but, through a combination of passive and active measures, to radically reduce its power and to make it simply another international institution coexisting with and being checked by other international organizations, agreements, and regional groupings. These would include such diverse actors and institutions as UNCTAD, multilateral environmental agreements, the International Labor Organization (ILO), evolving trade blocs such as Mercosur in Latin America, SAARC in South Asia, SADCC in Southern Africa, and ASEAN in Southeast Asia.

It is in such a more fluid, less structured, more pluralistic world with multiple checks and balances that the nations and communities of the South will be able to carve out the space to develop based on their values, their rhythms, and the strategies of their choice.

NOTES

1. Press briefing, Seattle, December 2, 1999.

2. Quoted in "Deadline Set for WTO Reforms," Guardian News Service, Jan. 10, 2000.

3. Figures from World Trade Organization, Annual Report 1998: International Trade Statistics (Geneva: WTO, 1998), p. 12.

4. Quoted in "Cakes and Caviar: The Dunkel Draft and Third World Agriculture," Ecologist, Vol. 23, No. 6 (Nov.–Dec. 1993), p. 220.

5. C. Fred Bergsten, Director, Institute for International Economics, Testimony before U.S. Senate, Washington, DC, Oct. 13, 1994.

6. UNCTAD, *Trade and Development Report 1991* (New York: United Nations, 1991), p. 191.

7. See discussion of this in Walden Bello and Stephanie Rosenfeld, *Dragons in Distress: Asia's Miracle Economies in Crisis* (San Francisco: Institute for Food and Development Policy, 1990), p. 161.

8. Quoted in John Whaley, "Special and Differential Treatment in the Millenium Round," CSGR Working Paper, No. 30/99 (May 1999), p. 3.

9. Ibid., p. 4.

10. Ibid., p. 7.

11. Ibid., p. 10.

12. Ibid., p. 14.

13. "More Power to the World Trade Organization?," Panos Briefing, Nov. 1999, p. 14.

14. South Center, *The Multilateral Trade Agenda and the South* (Geneva: South Center, 1998), p. 32.

15. John Whaley, "Building Poor Countries' Trading Capacity," CSGR Working Paper Series (Warwick: CSGR, March 1999)

16. Secretary of Trade Cesar Bautista, Address to 2nd WTO Ministerial, Geneva, May 18, 1998.

17. C. Fred Bergsten, Director, Institute for International Economics, Testimony before the U.S. Senate, Washington, DC, Oct. 13, 1994.

18. Ibid.

19. Ibid.

20. Press briefing, Seattle, Washington, Dec. 2, 1999

21. Ibid.

22. "Deadline Set for WTO Reforms," Guardian News Service, Jan. 10, 2000.

*T*he IMF and World Bank are the chief pushers of the whole schema of structural adjustments that are designed to further open up the Third World economies for penetration and plunder by private monopoly corporations. We call for the abrogation of all loan agreements that provide for structural adjustment, public assumption of private debts and the further exposure of the Third World economies to plunder by private multinational giants.

Cebu Declaration, Philippine-Asia Jubilee Campaign Against the Debt, May 18, 1999, Cebu City, Philippines

15

Spinning a New Mythology
WTO As the Protector of the Poor

Vandana Shiva

For the past five years, the primary justifications for the World Trade Organization (WTO) have been arguments about the inevitability of globalization and the argument of helplessness of the Third World in the face of a single super power (the United States).

As recently as March 1999, at a high-level Trade and Environment symposium, free trade theorist Fred Bergsten argued that we could not stop or reverse globalization because it was like a bicycle: if it stopped, we would fall. He had clearly not ridden a bicycle, because every bicycle rider knows that all you have to do to safely stop a bicycle is put your foot down.

That is what the citizens and Third World governments did in Seattle. They put their foot down and the machinery came grinding to a halt. All mythology of "natural phenomena" and "inevitability" evaporated in thin air.

Globalization is not like a bicycle; we can get off bicycles. It is more like the escalator which crushed an 8-year-old girl, Jyotsana Jethani to death at the Indira Gandhi International Airport on the morning of 13th December 1999 because it could not be stopped. Nobody knew how to switch the escalator off or where the switch was. The escalator ground to a halt only after it was jammed by the body of the child.

The WTO is building the world's economic and political architecture like the escalator. By dismantling regulations and trade restrictions, a system is being created in which no one knows where the switch is and who is responsible to switch it off. The rules of WTO are ensuring that neither local communities nor national governments can regulate trade or investment under free trade. Switches to the economic escalator are being taken out of our hands, and being put beyond our reach so that it cannot be stopped, even as ecosystems and people are crushed to death and people watch helplessly. Little Jyotsana symbolizes the fate of millions who are being crushed in the unstoppable machine of global free trade.

The protests in Seattle were about getting the switches to the global economy back in peoples hands and under democratic control to prevent total social and ecological breakdown. Seattle dispensed with the myth that globalization and free trade cannot be stopped or challenged. It also got rid of the argument that the U.S., as the only super power, would always have its way.

Firstly, the super power was under siege by citizens from across the world: farmers, women, young people, the environmental community and workers, and it behaved as brutally as any anti-people government does in the face of people's resistance. Seattle was the Tianamin Square of the U.S., and it was a leading Chinese human rights activist who made the analogy.

Secondly, the African, Caribbean and Latin American countries who had been totally excluded from the "green room" negotiations, also rebelled against the WTO and the U.S., and refused to be bullied any further.

Thirdly, even major players from the Third World such as India, whose government forced the Uruguay Round decisions on their citizens in spite of massive protests from farmers and workers throughout the 1990s, on the basis of the logic of the futility of standing up against a super power, took on the super power on the issue of trade sanctions linked to labor issues.

Now that the arguments of inevitability have lost their steam, new mythology is being spun to save the WTO. The WTO has suddenly been redefined as the ultimate institution of the poor, even though it is the poor who bear the highest social and ecological burden of WTO rules.

Mike Moore, the Director General of WTO claimed that the WTO protestors hurt the poor and the marginalized. "who are looking to us to help them."[1] Markose Arackal says "The events in Seattle have put a serious question mark on the ability of the World Trade Organisation in the near future anyway, to deliver a more liberal trade regime to the world's poor nations. And that may rob us of the surest way to get rich fast, and remove widespread poverty in our part of the world."[2] Swaminathan Anklesaria Iyer has declared WTO the protector of India, the TNCs as India's "natural allies" and citizens groups as the "real enemies" of the Third World.[3]

Politics and power is being redefined. The powerful of the world—in governments, politics, media and business—are emerging a new global alliance, transcending North-South divides. This global alliance of the powerful sees people, people's organizations and NGO's as the biggest threat, both domestically and internationally. This is the core of Swaminathan Iyer's argument of TNCs as "natural allies" and NGOs as "real enemies."

A society in which people are the enemy and colonizers are friends is a colonized society; it is a society in which freedom has been destroyed for people and the nation. It is a society which is enslaved. The powerful elites are institutionalizing slavery through the WTO. The WTO as the institution of the poor is a new mythology being spun, not to protect the poor, but to protect the WTO and TNCs, and hence perpetuate the trade rules which are the ultimate assault on the survival of the poor.

Trade liberalization is dismantling the last protections of the poor—and robbing their last resources. For the thousands of farmers in India who have been pushed to commiting suicide due to indebtedness after the seed sector was opened up to TNCs, the economy has become like the Airport Escalator, consuming their very lives. For coastal communities whose lives have been devastated by the shrimp industry, for the small *ghanis* and oil mills and oilseed farmers whose markets have been snatched by imports of artificially cheap genetically engineered soya oil, the WTO is not a protector but a threat.

Our national elites have declared themselves "natural allies" of global corporations and are trying to transfer all our ecological and social wealth from the people to business and industry, including TNCs.

The announcement of the formation of eight working groups by the Indian Prime Minister under the leadership of businessmen and traders is part of this hijack of the nation and the total exclusion of citizens from the making of public policy including vital areas such as food, health and education.

The privatization of institutions of higher learning will soon be followed by globalization of education. One of the U.S. proposals for the WTO Seattle meeting was to enlarge services in the General Agreement on Trade in Services (GATS) to include health and education, transform them from being fundamental rights into freely traded commodities, accessible on global markets for those who have the purchasing power. This clearly leaves the large majority without access to basic needs and will push millions out of jobs and livelihoods.

The national elites have formed a new alliance with global corporations. They want and need the WTO because WTO rules offer them protectionism from the people and insulation from democracy, and it is people and democracy that the elite are most afraid of. The WTO rules allow them to bypass India's constitution and the fundamental rights that it embodies. WTO protects the elite of India and their global allies from the people of India. It does not protect the poor of India.

The new mythology of the WTO as the protector of the poor will not convince the millions who are paying for globalization and free trade with their very lives.

NOTES

1. *Business Standard*, December 2, 1999.
2. *Financial Express,* December 9, 1999.
3. *Times of India*, December 12, 1999.

16

Will a Social Clause in Trade Agreements Advance International Solidarity?

David Bacon

The AFL-CIO is calling for incorporating the rights of working people around the world into the text of future trade agreements, and for treating the impact of trade on workers as a fundamental issue.

But the AFL-CIO is proposing a way of dealing with trade with which a number of unions disagree. It proposes a social clause, which would incorporate into future trade agreements core labor standards, including prohibitions against child labor and prison labor, against discrimination, and against violations of the right of workers to organize unions and bargain. The WTO enforcement process, now used to protect the ability of transnational corporations to move investments and production freely across borders, could then be used to protect workers' rights as well, the labor federation argues.

But many unions, including left-wing ones in Europe and Canada, have serious questions about the proposal for a social clause. Some equate it with proposals in Europe to make a social contract between labor and capital part of the process of creating a single European economy.

The social contract has tended to be a proposal of Europe's more conservative unions. The more radical ones have argued for opposing the process of merging economies itself, rather than negotiating worker protections within an economic framework dominated by transnational corporations and banks. In Europe, the movement towards a single currency and the merger of markets has brought with it austerity formulas for the elimination of social benefits and protections won by workers over the last fifty years.

Social democrats are now in power in Britain, France, Germany and Italy. In some of those countries workers and unions have been able to reverse the economic trend, and some governments have been more responsive to worker pressure than others. But all these social democratic governments argue that for Europe to make it in the world economy, productivity has to be increased, and social needs and benefits brought into line. That often brings the governing parties into basic conflict with the working-class base which has brought them to power. The conflict is not so different from that which has taken shape in the U.S. between labor and the Clinton administration.

The flaw in the social democratic argument is that its assumption and purpose is wrong. Society exists to serve the social needs of people, not the productivity needs of capital. Those two needs are in basic conflict—a conflict of class interest.

The criticism made by the Canadian Labour Congress of the proposal for a social clause in the WTO negotiations is similar. "The struggle by unions, social justice groups and environmentalists is about more than just winning a seat at the table, or a 'social clause' or environmental rules," a CLC statement declares. "We're determined to change the entire trade regime."

But even assuming that negotiating a social clause is a good idea, in the context of trade negotiations first of all it requires that labor agree on a common agenda. The social clause the AFL-CIO proposes reflects the institutional needs of unions in a wealthy, industrial country. Unions and labor in other countries see other needs as well, especially the need for economic development. Parents of farmworker families in the Philippines and Mexico, for instance, overwhelmingly agree they would prefer that their kids had the opportunity to go to school rather than work. But simply prohibiting child labor doesn't provide that opportunity. It just cuts the income the family depends on to survive.

Labor federations in developing countries propose a large variety of programs for economic development. The more conservative generally support foreign investment and the governments which encourage it. The more radical ones support a program of national development which seeks to protect local industries, and even keep them in public, rather than private, hands. Those kinds of development programs are the antithesis of the economic framework the WTO enforces. Unless the international trade structure is changed drastically, these national development alternatives will not be possible. So proposing a social clause to limit the prerogatives of foreign investors lines up with the more conservative labor federations internationally, and undermines proposals for nationalization and national development less dependent on transnational capital.

Our definition of what the social clause should cover is narrow, reminiscent of the land reform proposals of the AFL-CIO in El Salvador during the civil war, or of the Sullivan Principles in South Africa. While labor rights are important, there's a bigger struggle going on over who controls the economies of developing countries, and what the development program is.

U.S. unions need to negotiate a common agenda with labor in developing countries, and recognize and respect differences of perspective and opinion. Saying, for instance, that the All China Confederation of Trade Unions is not a legitimate union body because it doesn't agree with the AFL-CIO's trade agenda is a form of national chauvinism, and smacks of the old coldwar prohibitions and destabilizations. It is also very short-sighted from the perspective of forging a common front against transnational corporations who seek to whipsaw workers and take advantage of differences in standards of living from country to country.

The big problem in the new (or old) international economic order is the difference in the standard of living between wealthy and poor countries. The difference between Mexico and the U.S., which was about 3:1 in the 1950s, is about 16:1 today. That difference is the cause of the loss of U.S. jobs as corporations relocate production. So long as this huge gulf exists, U.S. workers will continue to have that problem, social clause or no.

U.S. unions can seek to talk with the Chinese or Mexicans or Salvadorans or Cubans about the dangers they see in trying to rely on transnational corporations as a source of capital for economic development, and should do so. And of course, if they have fraternal, cooperative relationships based on mutual respect and self-interest, they will have a more receptive audience than they will if they treat people with whom they disagree as though they had no right to exist.

But the big problem isn't the policies of foreign labor federations, or even their governments, but with our own. U.S. economic and trade policy has a greater influence on the widening gulf in income than any other single factor, and that, of course, is our responsibility.

The Clinton administration, which at first was unwilling to discuss any labor protection, has seen a certain reality: addressing the worst of the abuses in foreign factories (whether in real or just PR terms) is a way of deflecting domestic pressure. But the White House has no interest in addressing the fundamental problem of poverty, and the role U.S. policies play in perpetuating it. In fact, if anything, Clinton's newfound interest in labor standards is a way of enabling the implementation of those same policies. So the Labor Department proposes a garment code of conduct which prohibits forced and unpaid overtime after 60 hours, or the labor of kids under 14, in Central American sweatshops. The corporations which violate the code are demonized, and the ones that don't are considered okay.

But the proposals for standards and codes of conduct leave unasked a basic question: Where does the poverty come from which forces workers through the factory doors? What policies are pursued by the U.S. government which perpetuate that poverty? Seeking to avoid these questions, the administration proposes to negotiate over limits on the worst abuses (not necessarily as the workers of those countries define them), so long as U.S. labor basically accepts an international trade structure and economic order which institutionalizes the gulf in the standard of living, and the impoverishment of whole nations.

An alternative program for international labor solidarity could be based on a much broader set of ideas. They might include:

1. Negotiate an agenda (including the terms of social clauses), based on mutual respect and self-interest, with the unions and workers of all countries.

2. Accept the legitimacy of existing unions—no Cold War prohibitions or destabilization programs. Develop friendly and cooperative relationships based on dealing with common employers, and with the effect of U.S. trade and economic policies on the people of the country involved.

3. Oppose the negotiation of new trade agreements, and demand the restructuring of the international economic order.

4. Make international policy dealing with the difference in standards of living from country to country a primary objective of AFL-CIO policy, reexamining the role U.S. economic, political and military policy plays in reinforcing that difference. Labor solidarity means opposing U.S. foreign policy in areas where it has led to drastic decline in living standards, such as the economic reforms in eastern Europe.

5. Make independence from U.S. foreign policy a matter of principle, including ending subsidies for AFL-CIO programs from the U.S. Agency for International Development, the National Endowment for Democracy or other government institutions. The AFL-CIO should be unafraid to publicly criticize imperial policies like the U.S. counterinsurgency program in Colombia, economic and military sanctions in Iraq and Serbia, and the economic blockade of Cuba.

17

The WTO Turns Back the Environmental Clock

Environmental Research Foundation

The World Trade Organization (WTO) has effectively canceled the three mainstays of modern environmental protection: (1) pollution prevention using bans, (2) the precautionary principle, and (3) the right-to-know through labeling. In effect, the WTO has erased thirty years of work by environmental activists and thinkers, forcing us back to an earlier era of "end of pipe" pollution regulations based on risk assessment.

Starting in the mid-1960s, the U.S. Congress created a pollution control system based on risk assessments and "end of pipe" regulations. As evidence of harm accumulated (a process sometimes called "lining up the dead bodies"), the government conducted risk assessments to decide how much toxic pollution was acceptable. Corporations then added filters and scrubbers to reduce their harmful discharges to "acceptable" levels.

Large corporations learned to live with this system; they even turned it into a competitive advantage. As the number of regulations multiplied, large polluters hired staffs of lawyers and engineers who did nothing but worry about the regulations. Small corporations could not afford to hire specialists to formally participate in rule-making procedures, compliance disputes and lawsuits. For small firms, compliance became a paperwork nightmare and a burdensome expense. Big firms learned to thrive under the rules.

Under the end-of-pipe, risk-based regulatory system, regulations were always a compromise between what the scientific data indicated and what the corporate polluters were willing to accept. Regulatory officials would propose a numerical standard based on risk assessments, the corporate experts would challenge the proposal, and ultimately a regulation would emerge that was a compromise between the two positions. Obviously, such a system could never fully protect public health or the environment.

Large corporations had one additional advantage in these regulatory negotiations: they were sitting across the table from a government bureaucrat who was underpaid and often overworked. After the regulatory negotiations were finished, the corporation might offer the government official a well-paid position as "Vice-President for Environmental Compliance." Knowing that the future might bring such a job offer, regulatory officials were inclined to play ball with the polluters. In fact, government officials went to work for the polluters so frequently that the practice earned a special name: the revolving door.

In sum, large corporations learned how to make the regulatory system work for them. But the system never worked well to protect the environment. In fact, during three decades of environmental protection based on risk assessments and end-of-pipe regulations, the entire planet became contaminated with low levels of industrial poisons. Persistent organic pollutants like DDT, PCBs, and synthetic compounds of lead and mercury found their way to the deepest parts of the oceans, to the highest mountaintops and to the most inaccessible reaches of the poles. No place on Earth remained pristine. As these exotic poisons entered food chains, they collected in the bodies of the largest predators, chief among them humans. As a result, even today if human breast milk were bottled and offered for sale it would be subject to ban by the U.S. Food and Drug Administration as unfit for human consumption. (Despite the presence of low levels of industrial poisons, breast milk is still far healthier for a baby than any alternative.)

During this period, the incidence of childhood cancers increased at the rate of about one percent per year. Immune system disorders in children, such as asthma, increased even more rapidly. Many observers of the regulatory dance began to believe that bathing our children in industrial poisons was not such a good idea, so new principles of environmental protection were invented:

1) In the early 1960s, true pollution prevention was born. The U.S. banned above-ground nuclear weapons tests to eliminate radioactive fallout. By the mid-1970s, the atomic fallout precedent was being applied to banning DDT, PCBs, leaded gasoline and several other dangerous toxicants. Bans are the essence of pollution prevention. But bans leave no wiggle room for the polluters.

2) The precautionary principle. In 1976, the U.S. Congress voted against a proposal to create a supersonic transport airplane (the SST). Based on evidence suggesting that the SST might harm the upper atmosphere and might lay down a swath of "sonic booms" everywhere it flew, Congress took precautionary action and voted down the SST proposal.

The precautionary principle moves the burden of proof of safety onto the proponents of a new project, a new technology or a new chemical. The public does not have to "line up the dead bodies." Instead the polluters have to convince the public and the government that the number of dead bodies in future will be acceptably small. In simplest terms, the precautionary principle says, "Better safe than sorry," the complete opposite of risk-based regulations.

Corporate polluters resent this innovative approach because now they must bear the burden of proof of safety. Their hands are tied unless they can convince the public and the government that their next innovation will be acceptably safe.

3) Eco-labeling. Labels on cans of tuna fish now say "dolphin-safe." Many products in the grocery store now say "organically grown." Some types of paper say "recycled." Labels that say "Made in Burma" signal that this product may have been made with slave labor. Such labels represent a market-based ap-

proach empowering people with information so they can vote with their dollars to protect the things they value. In essence, eco-labeling says people have a right to know the effects of their purchases on the natural environment, on their health, and on society. However, an informed citizenry can threaten corporate dominance.

Thus all three of these modern principles are unsatisfactory from the viewpoint of large corporations because they shift the advantage to the public in protecting health and environment. They impose societal values on the economy.

To get rid of these troublesome new principles of environmental protection and to force the world back to end-of-pipe regulatory controls based on risk assessments, corporations have now created the WTO. In only five years of operation the WTO has gone a long way toward declaring each of these three principles illegal. Now, according to current WTO rules, the only legal system for pollution control is the old end-of-pipe system based on risk assessment.

WTO principles undermining environmental protection include these:

1) WTO rules say that the method of production cannot be used as a basis for discriminating against a product. The WTO has formally established this principle in several decisions. When the U.S. refused to allow the importation of tuna fish caught in nets that needlessly killed millions of dolphins, Mexico took it to the GATT (the predecessor of the WTO) and won. The ruling said it was not legal to discriminate against canned tuna based on the methods by which the tuna was produced. Since then, the WTO has reaffirmed this principle several times.

As Ralph Nader's Public Citizen has written:

"The ability to distinguish among production methods is essential to environmental protection and environmentally sensitive economic policies... Trade rules that forbid the differentiation between products based on production methods make it impossible for governments to design effective environmental policies."

The WTO has effectively tied governments' hands—a corporate polluter's dream.

2) Restrictions on goods must be the least trade-restrictive possible and the restrictions must be "necessary." To prove that a regulation is "necessary," a country must prove that there is a worldwide scientific consensus on the danger, and a WTO tribunal of corporate lawyers must agree that the proposed regulation is a reasonable response to the danger. Furthermore, any regulation must be the "least trade-restrictive" regulation possible. Obviously, this puts an almost insurmountable burden of proof on any government wanting to protect its citizens and its environment from harm. Thus the WTO has shifted the burden of proof back onto the public. The dead bodies must be lined up once again.

The effect of these rules is that a product cannot be banned. It can be regulated using risk assessment but it cannot be banned. This was first established when the European Union (EU) tried to ban the import of U.S. meat which has been treated with hormones, some of which are carcinogenic. The Europeans said there was evidence that certain hormones can cause cancer (which is true) and they said they wanted to set a "zero-risk" standard for their citizens for this hazard.

The Clinton/Gore administration challenged the European ban before a WTO tribunal. The WTO ruled that the Europeans did not have a scientific risk assessment that showed convincingly that a zero-risk standard was warranted. That opened the door to ending all bans.

Now France wants to ban asbestos, but is being challenged by Canada on several grounds; one is that there is no worldwide scientific consensus that a ban is warranted. Denmark has announced its intention to ban 200 lead compounds, but the Clinton/Gore administration is challenging this as illegal because there are less trade-restrictive ways to achieve the same public health objective, Mr. Gore says. The European Union has said it wants to ban lead, mercury and cadmium in electronic devices, but the Clinton/Gore administration is challenging this before the WTO.

Mr. Gore's position is that bans are illegal restraints on trade and that regulations based on risk assessment are the only legal way to control environmental hazards. There is ample precedent for this position in WTO decisions.

3) Labeling—even voluntary labeling—is on the way out. The European Union has now passed a law requiring food containing genetically modified organisms to be labeled as such. The Clinton/Gore administration has said formally that this is an illegal restraint of trade because there is no difference between normal food and genetically modified food. (But if there were no significant differences, the U.S. Patent Office could not legally issue patents for genetically modified foods. And such patents are now routinely issued.)

When the EU refused to allow hormone-treated meat from the U.S. to be sold in Europe, their fallback position was that they might allow the sale of hormone-treated meat if it were clearly labeled. The Clinton/Gore administration says this would illegally discriminate against U.S. meat by labeling it according to its method of production.

The Clinton/Gore administration officially argues that even "country of origin" labels are WTO-illegal because they allow consumers to discriminate against certain countries (like Burma with its propensity for slave labor). The WTO has not yet ruled that "eco-labels" are illegal, but the handwriting on the wall is very clear. It appears to be only a matter of time before the modern era of environmental protection is fully rolled back.

It also appears that the only way to protect the environment in future will be to dismantle the WTO.

Notes

(1) Lori Wallach and Michelle Sforza, *Whose Trade Organization?: Corporate Globalization and the Erosion of Democracy* (Washington, D.C.: Public Citizen, 1999).

(2) Jim Puckett, *When Trade Is Toxic: The WTO Threat to Public and Planetary Health* (Seattle: Asia Pacific Environmental Exchange and Basel Action Network, 1999). Available from www.ban.org; Basel Action Network, c/o Asia Pacific Environmental Exchange, 1827 39th Ave. E., Seattle, WA. 98112.

18

A New Food Movement
Comes of Age in Seattle

Peter Rosset

An emergent global food movement figured prominently in the week-long Battle of Seattle. From Brazilian landless rural workers to students dressed as Monarch butterflies to protest genetically engineered (GE) corn that releases pollen lethal to this fragile species, food and farming often took center stage in Seattle.

It has been a quarter century since activism first crystallized so clearly around our food system. Then, Frances Moore Lappé wrote *Diet for a Small Planet* and founded Food First/The Institute for Food and Development Policy. The essential contribution of *Diet* to our political discourse was the understanding that food is at once personal and political: personal, in that the food we eat or can't afford to eat affects our bodies, our health, and carries our cultures encoded within it; and political, because who eats and who doesn't is determined by political power, and becuase every time we shop we make profoundly political choices. As our hand moves from one item on the supermarket shelf to another, do we choose an organic product grown by a local family farmer or by unionized farmworkers, or do we choose something that has been flown halfway around the world by a global food conglomerate?

If we make the latter choice, we might ask some of the following questions: Which indigenous farmers were displaced from their ancestral lands and stopped growing food for their communities so the land might be used for export crop production to provide us with fresh grapes or broccoli out of season? What pesticides were used to produce it, who was poisoned by them, which fishery was destroyed, and what residues remain when I eat it? What altered genetically material does it contain, and what largely unknown health and environmental risks does that entail? Which American farmers where driven out of business by this cheap import? How much ozone was destroyed and how much petroleum wasted, so a refrigerated ship might bring it to us fresh? Which transnational corporation holds the largest global market share of this commodity, and why do they generally get 70 cents of my consumer dollar when I buy it, and the farmer less than a penny? What farmworker unions and food processing unions did they bust?

At the start of the millennium, food, like no other issue, has the ability to draw together many groups that have more often than not been at each other's throats. In Seattle we saw alleged 'competitors' for markets, such as American farmers and Third World peasants, marching together as companions in struggle. Said one Wisconsin farmer, "the WTO fight in Seattle woke a lot of American farmers up to the fact that their fight isn't with farmers in France or India. The fight's with agribusiness and the whole corporate vision of forcing small farmers off the land."

American farmers also marched with environmentalists who in the past were seen as antagonists because of the productionist myth that food and jobs are incompatible with environmental concerns. Their common anger over GE crops brought these strange bedfellows together, farmers because they can't sell their altered grain and they feel the monopolistic power of the Monsantos of the world, and evironmentalists because of the risks posed by the new GE organisms. Consumer groups marched with farmers too, as did farmworkers and industrial unions in the food industry. Among the most excluded in our corporate controlled global food system are the inner city hungry in America and the rural landless in the Third World. They were there too.

Food clearly is an issue we can all rally around—we all eat—and all of our lives are profoundly touched by the politics of food. But why did it take Seattle and the WTO for the food movement to come together?

First, it is the growing corporate penetration of the global food system that leaves so many of us without what we need—whether we are middle-class consumers wanting safe, healthy food; small farmers trying to cling to the land; the landless or the hungry or consumers concerned about pesticides and altered harvests. Second, increasingly out-of-control free trade policies are a key element in the enormous jump in the corporate concentration of ownership in the food system over the last decade, and in the loss of family farmers worldwide. And finally, current and proposed WTO rules lock in those free trade policies and the system of corporate control over food. They do that by:

• Forcing countries to remove barriers to agricultural imports, driving down farm prices and bankrupting local farmers.

• Stopping governments from subsidizing their small and family farmers, eliminating social safety nets.

• Pushing countries to compete in the global economy based on low wages, union busting, cheap production costs, and weak environmental laws.

• Extending U.S.-style patents over life forms worldwide, allowing corporations to commodify genetic plant resources that were once the heritage of local communities.

• Making it difficult for countries to restrict the import of GE foods and seeds.

Family Farms and Free Trade

The specific example of how small farmers in the U.S. and other countries are hurt by corporate-driven free trade policies is illustrative of what is happening; similar damage is also being done to consumers, workers and the environment.

Over the past couple of decades Third World countries have been encouraged, cajoled, threatened, and generally pressured into unilaterally reducing the level of protection offered to their domestic food producers in the face of well-financed foreign competitors. Through participation in GATT, NAFTA, the World Bank, the International Monetary Fund and the WTO, they have reduced or in some cases eliminated tariffs, quotas and other barriers to unlimited imports of food products. On the face of it, this might sound like a good thing. After all, more food imports might make food cheaper in poor, hungry countries, and thus make it easier for the poor to obtain enough to eat. However, the experiences of many countries demonstrate that there are severe downsides to these policies that outweigh potential benefits.

Typically, Third World economies have been inundated with cheap food coming from the major grain exporting countries such as the United States. For a variety of reasons (subsidies, both hidden and open, industrialized production, etc.) this food is more often than not put on the international market at prices below the local cost of production. That drives down the prices that local farmers receive for what they produce, with two related effects, both of which are negative.

First, a sudden drop in farm prices can drive already poor, indebted farmers off the land over the short term. Second, a more subtle effect kicks in. As crop prices stay low over the medium term, profits per acre stay low as well. That means the minimum number of acres needed to support a family rises, contributing to the abandonment of farm land by smaller, poorer farmers. This land then winds up in the hands of the larger, better off farmers who can compete in a low-price environment by virtue of owning large acreage. They overcome the low profit per acre trap precisely by owning vast areas which add up to good profits in total, even if this represents very little on a per acre basis. The end result of both mechanisms is the further concentration of farm land in the ever fewer hands of the largest farmers.

A penalty is paid for this land concentration in terms of productivity, as large farmers turn to monocultures and machines to farm such vast tracts. And in terms of the environment, these large mechanized monocultures come to depend on agrochemicals. Jobs are lost as machines replace human labor and draft animals. Rural communities die out as farmers and farm work-ers migrate to cities. Natural resources deteriorate as nobody is left who cares about them. Finally, food security is placed in jeopardy: domestic food production falls in the face of cheap imports; land that was once used to grow food is placed into production of export crops for distant markets; people now de-pend on money rather than land to feed themselves; and fluctua-tions in employment, wages and world food prices can drive millions into hunger.

Via Campesina is an umbrella organization that brings to-gether small farmer associations and unions from around the world. Their statement released in Seattle underscores these prob-lems:

> *Via Campesina* rejects the neoliberal policies that push countries into cash crop export production at the expense of domestic food production. These policies contribute to low commodity prices that are far less than the real costs of production. Developing countries are forced to adopt these policies in order to pay their external debt. These countries must also open their borders to the importation of food which leads to even greater debt. There is no doubt that the WTO is an instrument that places greater control and profits in the hands of the transnational corporations.

This is a more or less familiar process to North Americans, who have seen low crop prices and the 'get-big-or-get-out' men-tality of government policies that have driven four million farm-ers off the land since World War II. We have paid, and continue to pay, a heavy price with: runaway soil erosion from excessive mechanization and 'fence-row-to-fence-row' planting; urban problems because our inner cities can't absorb the excess labor expelled from rural America; and the general collapse of rural communities.

The major drive to export grain from America's heartland, which began in the 1970s, contributed to a 40 percent increase in soil erosion in the corn and soybean belts. Today about 90 percent of U.S. cropland is losing topsoil faster than it can be re-placed. The export boom also contributed to a 25 percent in-crease in average farm size, which was accompanied by the loss of one third of all American farmers between 1970 and 1992. The average American farmer has not benefited from the export boom. While U.S. farm exports jumped from less than $10 bil-lion to more than $60 billion per year, average farm income dropped by almost one-half. The profits have accrued to the gi-ant grain cartels, not to American farmers.

In a very real sense, the U.S. drive to dominate global grain markets has hurt family farmers and damaged rural ecosystems both at home and abroad.

What is euphemistically referred to as a "fair and market-oriented agricultural trading system"—almost totally free trade in farm products—is the agenda of U.S. government negotiators in the WTO. This represents the single gravest threat faced to-day by the world's rural peoples and ecologies. The further 'lib-eralization' of trade in agricultural products will mean greater freedom for the big to drive out the small, forcing people every-where to depend for their daily meals on distant global markets with unpredictable price swings. It also means another mass exo-dus from rural areas and the further growth of cities, and could lead to the final triumph of inefficient and ecologically destruc-tive monocultures over ecologically rational and sustainable farm-ing practices.

The Battle of Seattle offers unprecedented hope that we can stop these ruinous policies, that we may be able to build an inter-national food movement composed of farmers, workers, consum-ers and environmentalists—a broad global majority—with the political power to strike back effectively at corporations and the institutions that do their global dirty work.

Section Four

Ways to Restructure the Global Economy

It is one thing to criticize the existing institutions of the global economy; it is quite another to develop alternative institutions that can do a better job of managing the world's affairs. This section provides detailed proposals for how we can construct global economic institutions based on the life cycle instead of the money cycle.

William Greider starts off the section with "It's Time to Go On the Offensive." He lays out a number of legislative proposals for getting U.S. transnational corporations under citizen control so they can't destroy the environment and exploit workers the way they do now.

In "Trade Now, Pay Later," Steven Shrybman explores the intriguing question: What if we had an environmental regulatory body that had enforcement powers as strong as those of the WTO?

Walden Bello provides another *tour de force* in "UNCTAD: Time to Lead, Time to Challenge the WTO." Although the February 2000 UNCTAD conference in Bangkok did not amount to much, Bello makes a persuasive argument for the progressive role that could be played by this little known UN agency.

Veteran campaigner Robin Round makes the case in "Time for a Tobin Tax" that a small tax on international currency speculation is gaining support and could bring in huge amounts of funds that could be used for many social and environmental causes.

In "Rewriting the Rules for Global Investment," Tony Clarke shows that we can develop alternative criteria for the global economy.

Deborah James ("Fair Trade, Not Free Trade") contrasts the dominant economic ideology with an alternative system that is acquiring more and more supporters every day.

Global Exchange co-founder Kevin Danaher, in "Why and How to Pressure the World Bank," gives rationale and technique for attacking the Bank at the heart of its financing: boycotting the bonds that the Bank sells to raise most of its money.

In the Conclusion, "Ten Ways to Democratize the Global Economy," Deborah James provides a wide range of ways you can get involved in the movement for global transformation.

19

It's Time to Go on the Offensive. Here's How.

William Greider

The promise of Seattle was captured in an antic moment observed by one young environmental activist. Amid broad ranks of protesters, he saw that a squad of activists dressed as sea turtles was marching alongside members of the Teamsters union. "Turtles love Teamsters," the turtles began to chant. "Teamsters love turtles," the truck drivers replied. Their call-and-response suggests the flavor of this loose-jointed new movement—people of disparate purposes setting aside old differences, united by the spirit of smart, playful optimism. The corporate-political establishment doesn't get it yet, but sea turtles and Teamsters (with their myriad friends) can change the world. This popular mobilization, disparaged as "Luddite wackos" by the prestige press, is still inventing itself, still vulnerable to the usual forces that can derail new social movements. But its moment is here, a rare opportunity to educate and agitate on behalf of common human values. Among its tasks, this new movement can excavate the human spirit, buried by a generation of arrogant power and a brittle-minded economic orthodoxy.

So what's next for turtles and Teamsters? The World Trade Organization's failure at Seattle (gridlocked on commercial disputes, oblivious to the reform agenda from the streets) has in-

spired a new organizing slogan: "Fix it or nix it." The WTO is
the visible symbol of globalization, and the network of forty coun-
try-based campaigns that produced Seattle is working now on
when to stage another international day of action.

The U.S. coalition is, meanwhile, gearing up for another crucial fight: blocking Congressional action that would give China
a permanent "good housekeeping seal"—instead of annual ap-
proval of most-favored-nation status—as it joins the WTO. Any
genuine reform of the global system becomes far more difficult
if China is to be treated as a "normal" trading partner—one reason business is so anxious to win this one.

Beyond immediate battles, this new movement will sustain
itself and grow powerful only if it goes on the offensive—that is,
if it can tell a positive story about how the world will look if its
values prevail. It can do this with hard facts about the present
realities, facts that blow away the establishment's smug abstrac-
tions. It should propose concrete legislation—reform laws to be
endorsed at the community or state level and enacted by Congress. Not after years of diplomacy, but right now.

What follows is a rough draft of what this national legislation
might look like (based on conversations with some leading activists and my own reflections). The central principle is that
Americans have the sovereign power to impose rules on the behavior of their own American-based multinational corporations
(notwithstanding the WTO's pretensions). Congress did so in
1977 with the Foreign Corrupt Practices Act, which prohibits
corporate bribery in overseas projects. That law was passed in
response to public outrage over repeated scandals revealing that
major U.S. companies were buying foreign governments. Human rights abuses present in the global system are far more grave
than business bribes.

Since it's obvious that the WTO and other international fo-
rums have no intention of acting, Americans really have no moral
choice but to assert responsibility. After all, random brutalities
in the production system are done in our name and to our benefit
as consumers, shareholders and company managers. As the United

Students Against Sweatshops has demonstrated, when people learn the facts, moral revulsion follows. Famous brand names find themselves confronted by what they have long denied.

In addition to holding U.S. companies accountable, this first round of legislation should focus on empowering voiceless peoples on the other end of the global system—workers, civic activists, communities—mainly by providing them with the industrial information that will help them speak and act in their own behalf. That means collecting hard data from American companies on where and how they produce overseas. Why would the business cheerleaders object, since they claim globalization itself fosters free-flowing information and democratic values?

These initial proposals are deliberately modest in scope because reformers from the wealthy nations, especially the United States, must first establish their bona fide intentions. The objective is not to stymie industrial development in low-wage economies or to rewrite laws for other societies. Poorer countries are naturally skeptical of our high-minded motives, since they've had long experience with the power of American self-righteousness. If this movement is truly international, it will begin by convincing distant others (the citizens, if not their governments) that our commitment to common humanity is genuine.

If these modest measures succeed, however, they will draw a new map of the world—delineating factory-by-factory which multinational companies are actively subverting shared human values, which nations are truly trying to improve conditions for their people and which are merely participating in the exploitation. The map separates sheep from goats, culprits from victims.

The information is essential because it can set the stage for subsequent legislation that eventually establishes minimum standards for corporate behavior on environmental protection, labor issues and human rights. Then penalty tariffs or other measures could be aimed at the firms or nations that systematically pursue the low road, profiteering on human suffering and ecological despoliation. Trade reform can likewise reward and nurture those nations struggling to break free of the "race to the bottom."

Business will howl that these new measures would put it at a competitive disadvantage, just as they opposed the antibribery law as an intrusion on quaint customs in foreign lands. The impact will be quite marginal if one believes the companies' own lofty claims about their offshore production. In any case, as the world's main buyer of last resort, the United States has the market power to lead on these reform issues. Our trade diplomats should start lobbying Europe and Japan to join this effort because eventually public opinion will turn on any multinational producer that attempts to reap short-term profit by ignoring standards for humane conduct. Obviously, this is politics for the long haul and difficult at every stage. But none of the barriers are insurmountable if we have our values straight. The action can begin with simple, straightforward matters like fire prevention.

The Pro-Life Factory

In 1993 the worst industrial fire in the history of capitalism occurred at a mammoth toy factory outside Bangkok: 188 workers killed, 469 seriously injured. All but a handful were women, some as young as 13. They were assembling toys for American children: Sesame Street dolls, Bart Simpson and the Muppets, Playskool "Water Pets" and many other popular items.

The most macabre fact about this historic tragedy was that hardly anyone in America noticed, though the Kader Industrial Toy Company's production supplied famous U.S. brands like Fisher-Price, Hasbro, Tyco and Kenner, and retailers like Wal-Mart and Toys R Us. Indeed, the Thai death toll surpassed the most scandalous calamity in America's own industrial history—the Triangle Shirtwaist Factory fire of 1911—and resembled it in haunting detail. Fire exits were blocked or inadequate, doors were locked to prevent pilfering, flammable materials were stacked randomly on the shop floors. Not even the most rudimentary fire precautions were provided for this factory with 3,000 workers. Desperate women jumped from upper-story windows by the score, just as young American women had done eighty-two years before in New York City.

Nor was this event unique in industrializing Asia. In 1994 ninety-three were killed and 160 injured in a Zhuhai textile factory when a fire led to the collapse of the building. In 1993 eighty-seven women died in the Zhili toy factory fire in Shenzhen, China. At Dongguan, a raincoat factory burned in 1991 and killed seventy-two people. Also in 1993, a textile plant fire killed sixty-one women in Fuzhou province. "Why must these tragedies repeat themselves again and again?" the *People's Daily* in Beijing asked. China's *Economic Daily* blamed "the way some of these foreign investors ignore international practice, ignore our own national rules, act completely lawlessly and immorally and lust after wealth."

The factory fires continue to this day in Asia, though they haven't been quite as horrendous. These routine human tragedies provoke local protests and official investigations but somehow escape the attention of the U.S. media. One obvious cause of the fires is the so-called three-in-one factory design—peasant workers sleep in a dormitory on the top floor, with the factory and warehouse beneath them. When a fire starts, the women are trapped, often suffocated by noxious fumes. This arrangement is officially illegal in China but still widely used.

In June 1999, the Zhimao Electronics plant fire at Shenzhen left twenty-four dead and forty injured; the *China Labor Bulletin* described it as "a copycat of at least six similar fires in south China." Nineteen people, including five children, died in a furniture factory fire last spring at Nanyang. In August 1999, the largest apparel factory in Dhaka, Bangladesh's industrial zone, burned to the ground on a Sunday night in August (evidently without casualties). Firefighters reported the absence of any fire-safety system. In October 1999, factory fires in Guangzhou's Baiyun district and Zengcheng's Shitan county killed thirty-one women, according to the *South China Morning Post*. In 1998, five workers were killed and twenty-three injured at a toy factory in Shenzhen when two of the dorm's balconies collapsed.

We begin with this mundane subject because there is absolutely no mystery about how to build and operate a safe industrial factory protected against this ancient hazard. It costs a bit more, that's all. What's missing in the global system is the political will to punish those who are scoring easy profits by ignoring such long-established industrial standards.

Congress can start here. It should enact a law that prohibits entry for any goods made in a factory that is not independently certified as employing standard fire-prevention design and equipment. The target is not mom-and-pop sweatshops operating in back alleys but the vast industrial plants producing for major global companies. They can afford to do this. Because the safety issue is so clear-cut and the human losses so dramatic, the law should permit zero tolerance for firms that ignore prudent precautions.

Does that sound too burdensome for business or too intrusive on foreign sovereignty? Consider this: The Federal Aviation Administration routinely performs similar safety tasks for aircraft, both at home and abroad. The FAA inspects production of foreign-made components that go into Boeing airplanes, certifies the airworthiness of foreign-made airliners and examines the work done offshore at overseas repair centers. Would you fly on a jetliner that was not certified by the FAA?

In fact, there are numerous other matters in which the U.S. and other governments demand the right to inspect foreign production or the content and origins of imported goods before trade is permitted. If America has the power to protect U.S. patents and copyrights by investigating knockoff CD factories in Southeast Asia, it is surely capable of protecting the lives of low-wage workers who make the toys, shirts, shoes and electronics we buy. If other nations don't wish to accept those terms, we can buy shirts and shoes somewhere else.

This issue, simple as it sounds, goes right to the heart of how globalization is organized because it challenges the irresponsibility of the "virtual corporation," that model of efficiency widely praised by management experts. "Virtual" firms operate like the central brain of a nervous system, connected to far-flung networks of suppliers and capable of shifting contracts regularly from one subcontractor to another, with no fixed accountability. One can blame the foreign-owned suppliers who scrimp on fire safety or blame local governments that do not enforce their own laws. But the moral culpability ultimately resides with the multinationals that run this arrangement (and, by extension, with the people who buy their products).

Subcontractors cut corners recklessly because they are compelled to compete on price for the next contract—a continuing cost-cutting contest that drives standards downward and ensnares poor nations as a whole. If Thailand enforces its laws too vigorously, the factories pick up and move somewhere else—Vietnam or China or Bangladesh—where workers are even cheaper and officials more compliant. This flexible system describes the treadmill that frustrates progress in poorer economies. Pioneered in low-end sectors (apparel, toys), it is increasingly evident in high-end production (autos, aircraft, advanced electronics).

Simple morality requires that we throw a little sand in the treadmill. Elementary rules, set in law, would reverse the incentives for corporate managers. Otherwise, as price-conscious consumers, we are all responsible for what happens to those young people.

Eco-Justice Goes Global

In federal district court in New York City, 30,000 residents of Ecuador are suing Texaco for class-action damages to their health and local environment. The oil company's executives are accused of making a conscious decision to dump more than 16 million gallons of oil and toxic wastewater into the Amazon River over two decades: three times the size of the Exxon Valdez oil spill in Alaska. The plaintiffs include three indigenous tribes and are represented by a Philadelphia law firm.

Stay tuned—this is a fast-developing new front in the globalization of law enforcement. In recent years, inventive lawyers have revived a 200-year-old federal law (the postrevolutionary Alien Tort Claims Act) as the legal basis for foreign citizens to sue U.S. multinationals in U.S. courts for their environmental or human rights abuses overseas. Unocal is being sued by Burmese workers for alleged collaboration with forced labor and torture by SLORC, the hideously repressive government of Burma. Royal Dutch/Shell announced a new code of conduct on human rights hours before the family of Ken Saro-Wiwa filed a lawsuit alleging Shell's role in the Nigerian military's execution of Saro-Wiwa.

This doctrine of legal standing is a long way from being established in the courts, but these and other suits are attempting to hold companies liable for malpractices abroad and the deception of American consumers at home. Obviously, this is not what American business had in mind as "tort reform." But the legal risks are quite real for U.S. multinationals, according to Stanford's Armin Rosencranz, an authority on international environmental law. It also opens a promising new field for trial lawyers, who took on big tobacco and showed that significant reform is still possible despite America's stalemated politics. Reform legislation, both at the state and national level, can advance the cause by ratifying in law that foreign citizens have clear standing to sue U.S. companies in U.S. courts, thus preempting the Supreme Court's business-friendly conservatives.

At the same time, Congress could require the companies to provide hard, precise data on environmental damage to those foreign communities and citizens who are usually kept in the dark about what's being done to their surroundings. Information is powerful. That's why companies don't often volunteer it. Daniel Seligman, head of the Sierra Club's responsible-trade campaign, suggests a preliminary outline: Congress could enact legal requirements that U.S. multinationals disclose toxic releases at overseas production facilities that would parallel the existing laws for industry at home. When an oil or mining company plans to open a new project in a foreign country, it would have to prepare the equivalent of an "environmental impact" assessment and share it with the affected community. The company would be required to engage in open discussions on potential consequences, not just with the national government but with the people whose health and habitat are threatened.

Furthermore, multinationals and their affiliated producers would have to disclose an annual inventory of what exactly is being dumped into the river or ground, what emissions are released into the air and, of course, what toxics are inside the factory. This does not intrude on any country's pollution standards, but it does equip citizens to act for themselves.

As U.S. environmentalists have learned from long experience, the process of enforcing pollution standards can be torturously slow and incomplete if it relies solely on government agencies. Enactment of U.S. toxic "right to know" laws in the eighties was a crucial turning point. The information unleashed grassroots energies and compelled many companies to accelerate compliance. No one should imagine that poor people in Asia, Latin America or elsewhere are indifferent to what's happening to their local environment. The problem is that they usually have no voice in the matter.

Thus, a new law would embody two fundamental reforms: First, companies would be compelled to make full disclosure of their pollution, and, second, affected foreign citizens would have the right to sue them for damages in American courts.

"This has nothing to do with eco-imperialism," Seligman emphasized. "It simply holds our own firms accountable to our values. It's not dictating the levels of pollution, but it's giving communities, not just governments, the information they need to decide their own destiny."

This reform should further stimulate the development of international civil society and the rule of law, both of which the business establishment claims to want. Local citizens, alarmed by the despoliation, could seek expert help from established environmental groups elsewhere in the world. If the facts are truly alarming, they could hire a lawyer to represent them in American courts.

Where Are the Workers of the World?

When consumer activists targeted the wages and working conditions associated with Nike and other famous brands, Mattel decided to act on its own, before Barbie dolls got caught in the same cross-hairs. Half of the Barbies are now made in China, where labor conditions are notorious and Mattel uses 300 subcontractors, according to the Asian Monitor Resource Center. Mattel developed a detailed industrial code for its producers, prescribing standards for everything from injury rates to the number of bathrooms per 100 workers.

The three-member Independent Monitoring Council chosen by the company to oversee compliance includes economist Murray Weidenbaum, an antiregulation conservative and well-known apologist for business practices. PriceWaterhouseCoopers, the global accounting firm, was hired to audit. No one should be surprised that their first report, in November, covering three major factories in China and some others in three other nations, gave Mattel high marks. It describes the local managers as enthusiastic about correcting certain deficiencies.

Still, even Mattel's own handpicked inspectors were baffled by the payroll records at two Chinese plants—the accounting system for wages, hours worked, overtime paid. The monitoring committee admitted that it "experienced difficulty in verifying certain elements of the pay structure.... A large majority of workers ... expressed a lack of understanding of their pay stubs."

The workers, likewise, seemed unfamiliar with Mattel's "Global Manufacturing Principles," though the new standards were supposedly explained to them. The council noted that when some workers responded to questions, "it appeared that these were memorized answers." Nor were workers able to say much about free expression or complaints to managers. "Most of them were either not conscious or were reluctant to talk about the freedom of association or unionization issues," the report noted.

A less charitable explanation of the wage-and-hour confusion was provided by the Asian Monitor Resource Center in a March 1999 report on what its citizen investigators found at twelve Chinese toy factories, including several where Mattel is active. "During the peak season, not a single worker can leave the workplace after eight hours' work," the center reported. "Most workers in these toy factories work ten to sixteen hours a day, six or seven days a week.... Since most toy workers are paid by piece rate, they never receive overtime pay."

Corporate codes of conduct have led to some improvements, the center noted, including on fire safety. "However," the report added, "we still found numerous blatant violations of workers' basic labor and human rights—including flagrant violations of China's own Labor Law, even though many of the factories we investigated are subcontractors for [multinationals] having codes of conduct on paper."

The Asian center, for instance, found that the Tri-S factory in Dongguan, which it identified as a Mattel and Tyco supplier, was still operating a "three in one" factory that is ostensibly illegal. Three hundred workers slept on the third floor; the second floor was full of raw materials. The issue is not Mattel's sincerity. The question is whether Americans will allow enforcement of labor rights to be "privatized"—left to the moral judgments of individual companies—or whether these complex matters must be codified in law as clearly stated benchmarks, so that corporate claims can be tested by independent verification and, if necessary, challenged in courts of law. Even if one accepted any individual company's good intentions, that still leaves millions of peasant workers subject to low-road practices by thousands of other companies and their contractors, responding to fierce market pressures that cut costs at human expense.

The first weapon is disclosure. One can collect countless horror stories on several continents, but the lack of reliable, comprehensive information remains a central problem. The codes of conduct, of course, further confuse the picture, since brand-name firms develop PR campaigns around them, while still refusing access to independent investigators.

In fact, until quite recently, companies would typically not even reveal where their goods were made—much less how their workers were treated. Under pressure from student activists and universities, Nike folded last October. It disclosed the locations of forty-two of its 365 factories.

Once again, national legislation should start with simple stuff—requiring firms to disclose information that enables citizens here and abroad to check out corporate behavior, and giving private citizens and organizations the legal standing to sue for damages if companies falsify their reports to the U.S. government. Given the overbearing political influence of the multinationals, legal standing for private lawsuits is crucial.

This much we do know: The U.S. government cannot be trusted to enforce labor standards, since it has repeatedly failed to do so under already existing laws. One especially sickening example occurred in 1994 when Suharto still ruled Indonesia. The Clinton Administration certified the regime's improving labor policies—thus keeping Indonesia eligible for trade preferences—at the very moment Suharto was smashing a promising new labor federation, imprisoning scores of its brave leaders and charging them with subversion.

An initial labor code should, obviously, require all U.S. multinationals to identify the names and addresses of offshore factories and their subcontractor plants, the owners and principal investors. Next, the corporations would answer some fairly simple questions about each factory: the number of workers and what they make, the base pay for production workers, the factory's labor costs as a percentage of its value-added output.

Finally, for every production site, the company would be required to certify the existence of well-accepted labor standards or to explain why its factory ought to be granted an exemption. Does the workplace comply with the host country's own labor laws? Does it comply with the International Labor Organization's "core labor standards," guaranteeing the right to organize, forbidding child labor and forced labor? If not, why not?

A more controversial suggestion would require each company to attest that its industrial workers do at least receive a "living wage," that is, income sufficient to provide for basic subsistence in terms of their own country and culture—food, housing, clothing, health and education. If not, these powerful companies would have to explain why such a minimal benchmark for modern industrial life is too expensive for them.

No one can demand that American companies alter another society's laws and customs, but once again we are separating bad guys from innocent players. It is not always the foreign government that suppresses labor rights but sometimes American companies who insist on it. My favorite example is the U.S. semiconductor industry's production platform in Malaysia—famous names like Intel, Motorola, Texas Instruments, Hewlett-Packard. At their insistence, the electronics sector operates union-free, though Malaysia has vigorous, independent unions everywhere else.

A typical reaction is: Do these foreign workers really want or need our help? Despite sometimes harsh conditions, aren't they better off with the jobs and grateful? It is true that many of the young people in poor countries, entering industrial life for the first time, are quite bewildered by their new circumstances. They have migrated from the desperate poverty of rural villages, eager for wage incomes. Many of them do not even grasp what a union is, much less understand the broader rights accorded to workers elsewhere in the global system.

What many of them do understand, however, is that they are being exploited. They don't have to be told this by do-gooders from America. They know it from the sordid working conditions or from meager wages and their own disappointed hopes. That's why there are so many wildcat strikes—thousands of spontaneous strikes that occur regularly across developing nations, not organized by any unions but by workers themselves. Angry workers even strike in China, despite the real risk of imprisonment.

These sporadic, local protests are seldom mentioned in the U.S. press, but together they constitute an optimistic statement about our common humanity.

Freedom and Unfreedom

Nobel economist Amartya Sen begins his new book, *Development as Freedom*, with a provocative comparison: "The battle against the unfreedom of bound labor is important in many third world countries today for some of the same reasons the American Civil War was momentous." Is it possible that Americans are once again participating in an economic system that is half free, half unfree?

The question does not seem far-fetched when one examines more closely the predicament of the young women in many Chinese factories. Typically, they are recruited from remote villages by a government agency that collects a fee from them for the job. They must pay for their own travel, then place a "deposit" with factory managers, who will withhold their wages for the first month or two and frequently also take away the workers' official ID cards. Hired under three-year contracts, they cannot leave or jump to better jobs without losing their money and perhaps identity papers too. Their factory dorms are fenced and guarded, the workers cannot come and go freely, the stories of brutality by security guards are commonplace.

This is not slavery, to be sure, but it does resemble a sly form of indentured servitude, imposed on people who are powerless to resist its terms. What can be done to stop it? For starters, a serious Congressional investigation that digs into the ugly facts and calls on corporate CEOs to explain themselves would do more than embarrass industry. The American people, I believe, cannot bear the guilty knowledge of how their consumer trifles are produced, any more than they could live with knowledge of the racial caste system in America once the civil rights movement compelled them to confront it. This new movement has the same task of teaching and confronting.

The "enhancement of human freedom," Sen argues, "is both the main object and the primary means of development." Democracy and civil rights are thus central to economic progress, but the "unfreedoms" Sen describes involve much more than legal guarantees of free speech and religion or standards for powerful corporations. Poverty also enslaves lives. So do the still-existing, precapitalist feudal systems that deny individual aspirations in some countries. So do the social hierarchies that send adolescent girls to work in the factories while the boys go to school. These confining forces and others interact with the marketplace, which sometimes liberates people and sometimes uses unfreedoms for its own ends.

Human rights, in other words, pose the most profound challenge for reform because the issues go to the core nature of every society, and legislation alone cannot resolve them. Americans, above all, must remember to bring humility to this struggle. The promise of life expectancy, as Sen observes, is greater for people in some very poor nations than it is for African-American males in the United States. Our luxurious wealth, not just our values, is sometimes implicated in the unfreedom of others. As this new movement educates us about global realities, we shall see ourselves more clearly.

Reprinted with permission from the January 31, 2000 issue of *The Nation*.

The Spirit of Seattle is not only alive and well, it is a working relationship. The breath of fresh democratic air, even though mixed with the scent of offensive gas, imbued all who breathed deeply in Seattle with the dignity of a free people. Would it fade? Would we lose the clarity, strength, and optimism created by the mass of people coming together and facing off against the WTO? Not likely.

The Alliance for Sustainable Jobs and the Environment is growing. Those who are not formal members still feel they are a vital part of us and we feel their presence as well. Seattle confirmed that "There is nothing as powerful as an idea whose time has come."

Michael Evenson,
Alliance for Sustainable Jobs and
the Environment (www.asje.org)

20

Trade Now, Pay Later

Steven Shrybman

For activists who have been working to establish an international legal framework for the environment there is some good news and there is some bad news.

First the "good" news. In 1995 more than 100 nations endorsed an agreement that will have profound impacts on biodiversity, climate change and virtually every other major environmental issue. The agreement is binding and is armed with powerful enforcement measures to ensure that every member lives up to its obligations under the treaty.

Unfortunately, the bad news is that this international treaty will be an environmental disaster.

Can't guess which agreement this is? Here are more clues. The treaty wasn't established under the UN Environment Programme; instead it was the product of highly secretive negotiations conducted by public officials working hand-in-glove with the world's largest corporations. Nor is it explicitly about the environment. In fact the treaty rarely mentions the word and never even refers to biodiversity, climate change or desertification.

For those still wondering, this international "environmental" treaty is the General Agreement on Trade and Services (GATS) supervised by the World Trade Organization (WTO). While its proponents deny that it is anything more than a commercial agreement, their protests betray the dangerously myopic perspective they bring to economic and trade policy. The WTO's environmental relevance has also been obscured behind a smokescreen of jargon. In "trade-speak" environmental standards become "technical barriers to trade," food-safety regulations are "sanitary and phytosanitary measures" while the genetic commons becomes a system of "intellectual property rights." This also explains why its backers have been successful in denying the link between trade agreements and environmental concerns.

In broad terms, the WTO is designed to entrench "grow-now, pay-later" globalization by removing the power of governments to regulate corporate activity in the public interest. The result is that it will undermine our capacity to redirect current economic, development and trade policies towards a truly sustainable path.

Clear evidence of its impact can be seen in a number of successful trade challenges to environmental, conservation and food-safety regulations. Since the WTO was founded four years ago we have watched (its rules prohibit public participation) as the treaty's enforcement machinery has been wheeled into action to punish governments that flout its rules.

The growing list of casualties now includes European and Japanese food-safety measures, U.S. clean-air regulations and marine mammal conservation laws, aid and development treaties between Europe and a few impoverished former colonies, and Canadian cultural programs. And the list is likely to grow.

These trade disputes represent only the most visible conflicts between free-trade rules and the environment. Indeed, the most damaging effects of this new global regime occur out of sight. Governments quietly abandon laws protecting the environment, consumers, worker rights and conservation, rather than become embroiled in international trade disputes.

Lately, many environmentalists have come to realize that while they were plodding down the hallways of conference centers trying to negotiate international agreements to combat climate change, protect biodiversity or reduce hazardous-waste trade to poor nations, the ink was drying on an agreement that would only heap fuel on these ecological fires.

This is discouraging, but it is also instructive. The WTO's

authority depends on powerful enforcement machinery and in this regard it offers a model for environmental treaties. It proves that when governments are motivated, they will sign up to truly binding international agreements.

Any government that violates WTO rules is vulnerable to sanctions—often too severe for even the wealthiest nation to ignore. In the organization's first trade complaint (a challenge by foreign gasoline refiners to U.S. Clean Air Act regulations) the U.S. government was given two options: either remove the offending statute or face trade sanctions in the order of $150 million a year.

A similar fate befell European food-safety regulations last year when the WTO ruled that a European Community (EC) ban on hormone-treated beef violated several rules. The WTO ordered the EC to remove its import controls and, when it refused, authorized trade sanctions worth more than $125 million as the price of its defiance. Moreover, sanctions can be imposed against unrelated products—wherever they will be felt most. In addition, WTO cases are routinely heard, decided, appealed and resolved within a year. It would be impossible to find any other legal sanctions against government initiatives that are as quick and effective as these.

In contrast, international environmental agreements rarely use trade sanctions. Even in cases where they exist they represent only a pale imitation of the powerful enforcement regime built into the WTO. Agreements like the Framework Convention on Climate Change and the Biodiversity Convention don't include any enforcement mechanism other than moral persuasion. This lack of teeth explains why governments have resolutely ignored commitments they made when they signed these agreements at the Earth Summit in Rio nearly eight years ago. Ultimately, nation-states must face legally binding obligations if international environmental goals are to be met. This is where we need to tear several pages from the WTO text concerning enforcement.

Consider, for example, the enforcement provisions of the WTO Agreement on Intellectual Property Rights which were written to promote the interests of global pharmaceutical, biotechnology and media firms. Then imagine environmental goals being taken as seriously as patent rights. If the WTO were transformed into an organization that was as concerned about climate change as it is about the growth of transnational drug companies, we could have an Agreement on Trade-Related Measures To Combat Global Warming.

Such an Agreement could require all WTO members to:

• adopt domestic laws to stabilize greenhouse-gas emissions at 1990 levels;

• provide for customs inspection, seizure and disposal of goods that were produced in ways that violate the Agreement;

• establish criminal sanctions for any breach of the legislation or regulations mandated by the Agreement;

• authorize the use of trade sanctions, including cross-retaliatory measures—such as prohibiting the export of energy or energy products—against any jurisdiction that was in breach of its obligations under the Agreement.

It is a measure of how much work lies ahead that a proposal to treat climate change as seriously as pharmaceutical patents would no doubt be greeted with complete incredulity by the WTO. That's why it's critical that governments be pressed to explain why they consider patent protection a higher priority than global warming or biodiversity loss.

But what then do we do with trade and investment deals that are currently exacerbating ecological crises? Does the WTO need to be fundamentally overhauled? Or do proposals to delegate environmental issues to a new UN organization, such as a Global Environmental Organization, make sense? The answer depends on whether you believe that the environment can be isolated and protected from the main thrust of free trade policies. In fact, they are cut from the same cloth.

As conflicts between environmental and trade policy became too obvious to deny, free traders have pushed the environment debate to the margins within the WTO or isolated it entirely.

Current WTO head Michael Moore suggests that environmental issues don't belong in his agency and should be left to "specialized institutions" with the expertise to address them. He is hoping that most people won't appreciate how intimately inter-related trade and environmental issues really are. Of course we do need to strengthen the mandates of the international environmental institutions. But it is naive to imagine that this can happen outside the framework of international economic relations. Indeed, the isolation of these organizations from UN agencies like the World Bank and the WTO explains the marginal influence they have had.

The WTO is as much an environmental agreement as the Basel Convention on Transboundary Waste Shipments is a trade agreement. The distinction is artificial and serves only to defeat efforts to build a sustainable and integrated model for human development. Trade agreements must serve the goals of combating climate change, preserving biodiversity, assuring food security and protecting diversity. By the same token, international environmental agreements must integrate economic and environmental strategies if they are to be effective and durable.

The need for fundamental reform of the WTO is undeniable. But a supranational Global Environment Organization (GEO) could also play a supportive role by legitimizing the use of trade and economic sanctions. A GEO will have to be equipped with enforcement mechanisms very much like those of the WTO. Noncompliance would be greeted with sanctions every bit as certain, swift and substantial as those meted out by the WTO. Economic and trade sanctions might not always be necessary, but they'd have to be available just in case.

It is unlikely that Michael Moore can imagine a GEO to rival the power and influence of the WTO he now heads. Indeed, the challenge of establishing an effective international environmental regime will be no less daunting than transforming the WTO. Ultimately, this is because both agendas have precisely the same end point—a treaty to promote ecological and economic security for all peoples, rather than some grotesque notion of international trade built on perpetual growth.

21

UNCTAD: Time to Lead, Time to Challenge the WTO

Walden Bello

Two central institutions of the Northern-dominated system of economic global governance, the International Monetary Fund (IMF) and the World Bank, are undergoing a severe crisis of legitimacy and have, at least temporarily, lost their sense of direction. The South has the opportunity to seize the initiative, frame the terms of debate on the future of global governance, and push for the creation of institutions that will truly serve its interests. UNCTAD (UN Conference on Trade and Development) can serve as the catalyst for this process.

A Backward Glance

To envision a strategy for the future, it is essential to glance back at the past, to reclaim the best in UNCTAD's history and to avoid its mistakes. The place to begin this analysis is the period of decolonization in the 1950s and 1960s. The emergence of scores of newly independent states took place in the politically charged atmosphere of the Cold War, but although they were often split between East and West in their political alliances, Third World countries gravitated toward an economic agenda that had two underlying thrusts: rapid development and a global redistribution of wealth.

While the more radical expression of this agenda in the shape of the Leninist theory of imperialism drew much attention and, needless to say, condemnation in some quarters, it was the more moderate version that was most influential in drawing otherwise politically diverse Third World governments into a common front. This was the vision, analysis, and program of action forged by Raul Prebisch, an Argentine economist who, from his base at the United Nations Economic Commission for Latin America (CEPAL), won a global following with his numerous writings. Developed in the late 1950s and early 1960s, Prebisch's theory centered on the worsening terms of trade between industrialized and non-industrialized countries, an equation which posited that more and more of the South's raw materials and agricultural products were needed to purchase fewer and fewer of the North's manufactured products.

Moreover, the trading relationship was likely to get worse since Northern producers were developing substitutes for raw materials from the South, and Northern consumers, according to Engels' Law, would spend a decreasing proportion of their income on agricultural products from the South. Known in development circles as "structuralism," Prebisch's theory of "bloodless but inexorable exploitation," as one writer described it, served as the inspiration for Third World organizations, formations, and programs which sprang up in the 1960s and 1970s, including the Non-Aligned Movement, Group of 77, Organization of Petroleum Exporting Countries (OPEC), and the New International Economic Order (NIEO). It was also central to the establishment of the UN Conference on Trade and Development (UNCTAD) in 1964, which became, over the next decade, the principal vehicle used by the Third World countries in their effort to restructure the world economy.

With Prebisch as its first Secretary General, UNCTAD advanced a global reform strategy with three main prongs.

The first was commodity price stabilization through the negotiation of price floors below which commodity prices would not be allowed to fall.

The second was a scheme of preferential tariffs, or allowing

Third World exports of manufactures, in the name of development, to enter First World markets at lower tariff rates than those applied to exports from other industrialized countries.

The third was an expansion and acceleration of foreign assistance, which, in UNCTAD's view, was not charity but "compensation, a rebate to the Third World for the years of declining commodity purchasing power." UNCTAD also sought to gain legitimacy for the Southern countries' use of protectionist trade policy as a mechanism for industrialization and demanded accelerated transfer of technology to the South.

UNCTAD At Its Apogee

To a greater or lesser degree, the structuralist critique came to be reflected in the approaches of other key economic agencies of the United Nations secretariat, such as the Economic and Social Council (ECOSOC) and the United Nations Development Program (UNDP), and it became the dominant viewpoint among the majority at the General Assembly. Instead of promoting aid, UNCTAD focused on changing the rules of international trade, and in this enterprise it registered some successes.

During the fourth conference of UNCTAD (UNCTAD IV) in Nairobi in 1976, agreement was reached, without dissent from the developed countries, on the Integrated Program for Commodities (IPC). The IPC stipulated that agreements for 18 specified commodities would be negotiated or renegotiated with the principal aim of avoiding excessive price fluctuations and stabilizing commodity prices at levels remunerative to the producers and equitable to consumers. It was also agreed that a Common Fund would be set up that would regulate prices when they either fell below or climbed too far above the negotiated price targets.

UNCTAD and Group of 77 pressure was also central to the IMF's establishing a new window, the Compensatory Financing Facility (CFF), which was meant to assist Third World countries in managing foreign exchange crises created by sharp falls in the prices of the primary commodities they exported.

Another UNCTAD achievement was getting the industrialized countries to accept the principle of preferential tariffs for developing countries. Some 26 developed countries were involved in 16 separate "General System of Preferences" schemes by the early 1980s.

These concessions were, of course, limited. In the case of commodity price stabilization, it soon became apparent that the rich countries had replaced a strategy of confrontation with an evasive strategy of frustrating concrete agreements. A decade after UNCTAD IV, only one new commodity stabilization agreement, for natural rubber, had been negotiated; an existing agreement on cocoa was not operative; and agreements on tin and sugar had collapsed.

Right-wing Reaction and the Demonization of the UN

By the late 1970s, however, even such small concessions were viewed with alarm by increasingly influential sectors of the U.S. establishment. Such concessions within the UN system were seen in the context of other developments in North-South relations, which appeared to show that the strategy of liberal containment promoted by Washington's liberal internationalists, who held sway for most of the post-war period up to the late 1970s, had not produced what it promised to deliver: security for Western interests in the South through the co-optation of Third World elites. The United Nations system was a central feature of the demonology of the South that right-wing circles articulated in the late 1970s and early 1980s. In their view, the UN had become the main vehicle for the South's strategy to bring about the New International Economic Order. As the right-wing think tank the Heritage Foundation saw it, the governments of the South devoted "enormous time and resources to spreading the NIEO ideology throughout the UN system and beyond. Virtually no UN agencies and bureaus have been spared."

The South's effort to redistribute global economic power via UN mechanisms was viewed as a concerted one: Private business data flows are under attack internationally and by individual

Third World countries; proposals for strict controls of the international pharmaceutical trade are pending before more than one UN body; other international agencies are drafting restrictive codes of conduct for multinational corporations; and UNESCO has proposed international restraints on the press.

Especially threatening to the Foundation was the effort by the Third World to "redistribute natural resources" by bringing the seabed, space, and Antarctica under their control through the Law of the Sea Treaty, the Agreement Governing Activities of States on the Moon and Other Celestial Bodies (called the "Moon Treaty"), and an ongoing UN study and debate over Antarctica. Malaysian Prime Minister Mahathir Bin Mohamad, the principal architect of the effort to get the UN to claim Antarctica, told the General Assembly "all the unclaimed wealth of this earth" is the "common heritage of mankind," and therefore subject to the political control of the Third World.

Crisis of the UN Development System

As the 1980s unfolded, the North's drive to discipline the South escalated. Taking advantage of the Third World debt crisis, the IMF and the World Bank subjected over 70 countries to structural adjustment programs, the main elements of which were radical deregulation, liberalization, and privatization. This was accompanied by a major effort to emasculate the United Nations as a vehicle for the Southern agenda.

Wielding the power of the purse, the United States, whose contribution funds some 20–25 per cent of the UN budget, moved to silence NIEO rhetoric in all the key UN institutions dealing with the North-South divide: the Economic and Social Council (ECOSOC), the United Nations Development Program, and the General Assembly. U.S. pressure resulted as well in the effective dismantling of the UN Center on Transnational Corporations, whose high quality work in tracking the activities of the TNCs in the South had earned the ire of the TNCs. Also abolished was the post of Director-General for International Economic Cooperation and Development, which had been one of the few concrete outcomes, and certainly the most noteworthy, of the efforts of the developing countries during the NIEO negotiations to secure a stronger UN presence in support of international economic cooperation and development.

But the focus of the Northern counteroffensive was the defanging, if not dismantling of UNCTAD. After giving in to the South during the UNCTAD IV negotiations in Nairobi in 1976 by agreeing to the creation of the commodity stabilization scheme known as the Integrated Program for Commodities, the North, during UNCTAD V in Belgrade, refused the South's program of debt forgiveness and other measures intended to revive Third World economies and contribute to global recovery at a time of worldwide recession. The Northern offensive escalated during UNCTAD VIII, held in Cartagena in 1992. At this watershed meeting, the North successfully opposed all linkages of UNCTAD discussions with the Uruguay Round negotiations of the GATT and managed to erode UNCTAD's negotiation functions, thus calling its existence into question.

This drastic curtailing of UNCTAD's scope was apparently not enough for certain Northern interests. For instance, the Geneva-based Independent Commission on Global Governance identified UNCTAD as one of the agencies that could be abolished in order to streamline the UN system. The Commission's views apparently coincided with those of Karl Theodor Paschke, head of the newly created UN Office of Internal Oversight Services, who was quoted by *Stern* magazine as saying that UNCTAD had been made obsolete by the creation of the World Trade Organization.

UNCTAD on the Defensive

During UNCTAD VIII, the North pushed to limit UNCTAD's function's to "analysis, consensus-building on some trade related issues, and technical assistance." But even in this limited role, UNCTAD managed during the late 1980s and 1990s to perform indispensable tasks for the South. Among other things, UNCTAD's research and analytical work:

• showed that structural adjustment was leading to stagnation, not to the promised growth path promised by the World Bank and the IMF;

• underlined the crippling debt overhang that made any development impossible, and thus provided the intellectual ammunition for the Jubilee 2000 debt cancelation campaign;

• continued to remind the world that a great cause of the crisis of Third World countries was not their lack of liberalization but the plunging prices of their raw material and agricultural exports and the continuing deterioration of the terms of trade against them;

• pointed to the tremendous potential instability posed by unregulated global financial flows and the threat posed by the liberalization of the capital accounts of developing countries;

• emphasized the continuing critical role of activist state policies in sustaining development at a time when the reigning neoliberal ideology sought to reduce the state's role to providing the legal framework to promote the unfettered flow of goods and capital;

• underlined the many biases against developing countries of the GATT-Uruguay Round and showed how, when it came to such agreements as the Agreement on Agriculture and the Agreement on Textiles and Garments, the developed countries were not delivering on their commitments.

Together with the United Nations Development Program's *Human Development Report*, UNCTAD publications provided unassailable empirical evidence that globalization was spawning greater inequalities between and within countries. The annual *Trade and Development Report* served as a healthy antidote to the paeans to the free market and free trade coming out of the WTO and World Bank publications such as the *World Bank Development Report*.

Opportunity Awaits Seizure

The collapse of the Third WTO Ministerial in Seattle provides an opportunity for UNCTAD to reclaim a central role in setting the rules for global trade and development. But this cannot be on the basis of the old paradigm and old practices that have marked the UNCTAD approach. For example, the old assumption that underlay the Prebischian model that full integration of the developing countries into the world economy is the way to prosperity must be questioned in light of the many negative consequences of globalization which have become painfully evident. These include the dangers that accompany the loss of self-reliance in agricultural and industrial production owing to the volatility of the global economy, such as the erosion of food security in developing countries where agriculture focuses on export-oriented production.

This is related to the need for UNCTAD to incorporate many of the insights of ecological economics, which sees global trade, whether managed or free, as one of the key factors destabilizing the national and global environment. It must give serious consideration to the principle of subsidiarity in production and trade—that whatever can be produced locally with reasonable cost should be produced and traded locally—as a way of preserving or enhancing the health of both environment and society.

Ecological economics and feminist economics drive home the point that "efficiency" or the pursuit of reduction of unit cost—the driving value of neoclassical economics—must be questioned, if not displaced. UNCTAD must elaborate a new paradigm that subordinates narrow efficiency to the values of social solidarity, social equity, gender equity, and environmental integrity.

UNCTAD's analysis must also move away from an overwhelming focus on international trade as the key factor in development and pay greater attention to both the economic and social measures that would allow for greater reliance on internal markets, including asset and income redistribution, such as land reform, that would create the economically empowered citizen consumers that would serve as the engine of the local economy. The indispensable and necessary links between growth, national sovereignty, and social reform must be placed at the center of trade and development policy.

The absence of serious attention to internal social reform owes itself to a simplistic North-South view of international economic relations. But equally important, UNCTAD has been too long a club of Southern governments and states that are uncomfortable with the examination of their internal political and economic arrangements. UNCTAD, in other words, must see that its constituency goes beyond governments to include, more fundamentally, their citizens. Thus, UNCTAD must not only solicit input from civil society and non-governmental organizations but also open up its decision-making processes to them.

In this regard, the words of Rubens Ricupero, UNCTAD's managing director, apply not only to the WTO but to the organization he leads. Decrying the "persistent inability" of international organizations to engage civil society, he warns that the net result is that frustration, fears, and concerns finally find expression in a confrontational and sometimes violent attitude, often leading to disruption and a feeling of confusion.

There is a clear need to reach out to the concerned individuals and organizations, to offer them an opportunity to be heard by governments not only when they march and protest in the streets, to start a process of ordered and respected dialogue with those who want to debate the central issues related to trade, investment, financial crisis, job insecurity, and growing inequality inside nations and among them.

Moving to Center-stage

Institutional and analytical reinvigoration is essential if UNCTAD is to break out of the cage that the rich countries have fashioned for it and carve out a much more powerful role in trade and development issues. Also essential is the will and the vision to accompany this process.

In this regard, both the draft "Plan of Action" and "Bangkok Consensus" are disappointing. Both documents broadly adhere to the North's limiting UNCTAD's mandate to "research and policy analysis; consensus-building; and the provision of policy advice and technical assistance aimed primarily at capacity building." Such an approach does not go beyond the "positive agenda" of the last few years, which put the emphasis on enhancing, via technical advice, the capacity of developing countries in the context of WTO negotiations. That role was essentially one of holding the hands of developing country governments as they integrated into the WTO. It was also a role that led to UNCTAD being deployed as a "fixer" for the WTO in controversial issues, such as the way it was recruited to become part of a WTO working party on investment during the Singapore Ministerial in 1996 in order to legitimize the process of bringing investment into the jurisdiction of the WTO.

What UNCTAD should be doing, in the aftermath of Seattle, is challenging the role of the WTO as the ultimate arbiter of trade and development issues. UNCTAD should instead be putting forward an arrangement where trade, development, and environmental issues must be formulated and interpreted by a wider body of global organizations, including UNCTAD, the International Labor Organization (ILO), the implementing bodies of multilateral environmental agreements, and regional economic blocs, interacting as equals to clarify, define and implement international economic policies.

UNCTAD, in particular, should push to become not just a forum for the discussion of policies. UNCTAD should become, as Secretary General Ricupero put it, a "world parliament on globalization." But this should be a parliament with teeth, with actual legislative power and executive power in the nexus of trade, finance, development and environment. It was under the aegis of UNCTAD that international agreements on stabilizing commodity prices and setting up a Common Fund to support countries suffering from price fluctuations for their exports were forged in the 1970s. It was also negotiations carried out under the UNCTAD umbrella that led to the establishment of GSP's or preferential systems for Third World imports. This activist, decision-making role is one that UNCTAD must reclaim.

There are many areas that demand UNCTAD intervention,

but four in particular urgently demand broad global agreements.

• There is a crying need for such an agreement on the "Special and Differential Treatment" that must be accorded to developing countries in global trade, investment and finance. Such an agreement would specify both positive and negative measures to protect developing economies from the perils of indiscriminate liberalization, support their efforts to develop or industrialize through the use of trade and investment policy, and secure their preferential access to Northern markets. Such an UNCTAD-sponsored agreement would serve as an overarching convention that would guide the actions of the WTO, IMF, European Union and all other major international economic actors.

• UNCTAD could also play a key role in addressing the critical nexus of trade and environment. Together with the UN Environmental Program and UNDP, UNCTAD could lead in drafting an agreement specifying broad but binding guidelines and a pluralistic mechanism, involving civil society actors, that would judge the conflicting claims of the WTO, multilateral environmental agreements, governments, and NGOs.

• In light of the failure of the G-7 to seriously respond to the crying need for a reformed global financial architecture, UNCTAD should seize leadership in this area and forge an agreement among its 180-plus member countries that would put such a system in place. Such a system could involve Tobin taxes, regional capital controls, and national capital controls, and a pluralistic set of regulatory institutions—innovations that are necessary for global financial stability but which are resisted by the banks, hedge funds, the IMF and the U.S. Treasury Department.

• UNCTAD could also lead in forging a "New Deal" for agriculture in developing countries. The emphasis of such a convention would not be the integration of agriculture into world trade but the integration of trade into a development strategy that will put the emphasis on raising incomes and employment in the agricultural sector, achieving food security through a significant degree of food self-sufficiency, and promoting ecologically sustainable production.

UNCTAD in a Pluralistic System of Global Governance

All this is not to suggest replacing the WTO and the IMF with UNCTAD. But it does mean UNCTAD taking an active role in a process of reducing the powers of the WTO and the IMF.

It is not surprising that both the WTO and IMF are currently mired in a severe crisis of legitimacy. Both are highly centralized, highly unaccountable, highly non-transparent global institutions that seek to subjugate, control, or harness vast swathes of global economic, social, political, and environmental processes to the needs and interests of a global minority of states, elites, and TNCs. The dynamics of such institutions clash with the burgeoning democratic aspirations of peoples, countries, and communities in both the North and the South. The centralizing thrust of these institutions clash with the efforts of communities and nations to regain control of their fate and achieve a modicum of security by deconcentrating and decentralizing economic and political power. In other words, these are Jurassic institutions in an age of participatory political and economic democracy.

UNCTAD may not have the material resources of these institutions, but it has something that the billions of dollars of the World Bank and IMF could not buy: legitimacy among developing countries.

A vigorous UNCTAD that competes in the process of defining global rules for trade, finance, investment and sustainable development is essential in a pluralistic global economic regime where global institutions, organizations, and agreements complement as well as check one another. It is in such a more fluid, less structured, more pluralistic world with multiple checks and balances that the nations and communities of the South will be able to carve out the space to develop based on their values, their rhythms, and the strategies of their choice. UNCTAD has a critical contribution to make in the emergence of such a system of global governance.

22

Time for a Tobin Tax

Robin Round

On 23 March 1999 the Canadian Parliament voted to "enact a Tobin Tax in concert with the international community." For three intense months people from across the country had written letters, signed petitions, penned newspaper articles and spoken out at public meetings. And now we had won. Canada had become the first country in the world to declare that currency speculators must be stopped.

During that time campaigners ran into the same basic questions from ordinary people who were just beginning to hear about global currency speculation and to get some sense of its dangers. Here are some of the key concerns raised and our responses to them.

So what is currency speculation and why is it a problem?

The world of international finance has become a global casino where investors seeking quick profits bet huge sums around the clock. Unlike investments in goods or services, speculators make money from money alone. No jobs are created, no services provided, no factories built and no widgets produced.

Investors play the bond and currency markets, profiting from the minute-to-minute, hourly or daily fluctuations in prices around the world. And the game is big—$1.5 trillion is traded every day, 95 per cent of which is bet on whether currency values and interest rates will rise or fall. Traders make money either way and they thrive when markets are highly unstable, as they were in Southeast Asia in 1997.

International investment banks are the big winners, but the game has far-reaching impacts on the losers. As the Mexican, Southeast Asian, Russian and Brazilian financial crises demonstrated, an enormous human toll is extracted from the citizens of these countries when investors panic and run for the exits.

As national economies become more integrated, future financial crises are inevitable unless changes are made.

What is the Tobin Tax?

In 1978 Nobel Prize-winning economist James Tobin proposed that a small worldwide tariff (less than half of one per cent) be levied by all major countries on foreign-exchange transactions in order to "throw some sand in the wheels" of speculative flows. For a currency transaction to be profitable, the change in value of the currency must be greater than the proposed tax. Since speculative currency trades occur on much smaller margins, the Tobin Tax would reduce or eliminate the profits and, logically, the incentive to speculate. The tax is designed to help stabilize exchange rates by reducing the volume of speculation. And it is set deliberately low so as not to have an adverse effect on trade in goods and services or long-term investments.

How would a Tobin Tax benefit the global economy?

It could boost world trade by helping to stabilize exchange rates. Wildly fluctuating rates play havoc with businesses dependent on foreign exchange as prices and profits move up and down, depending on the relative value of the currencies being used. When importers and exporters can't be certain from one day to the next what their money is worth, economic planning—including job creation—goes out the window. Reduced exchange-rate volatility means that businesses would need to spend less money "hedging" (buying currencies in anticipation of future price changes), thus freeing up capital for investment in new production.

Tobin's proposed tax would not have stopped the crisis in Southeast Asia, but it could help prevent future crises by reducing overall speculative volume and the volatility that feeds speculative attack.

How would the Tobin Tax benefit national governments?

It is designed to reduce the power financial markets have to determine the economic policies of national governments. Traditionally, a country's central bank buys and sells its own currency on international markets to keep its value relatively stable. The bank buys back its currency when a "glut" caused by an investor selloff threatens to reduce the currency's value. In the past, most central banks had enough cash in reserve to offset any selloff or "attack." Not any longer. Speculators now have more cash than all the world's central banks put together. Official global reserves are less than half the value of one day of global foreign-exchange turnover. Many countries are simply unable to protect their currencies from speculative attack.

By cutting down on the overall volume of foreign-exchange transactions, a Tobin Tax would mean that central banks would not need as much reserve money to defend their currency. The tax would allow governments the freedom to act in the best interests of their own economic development, rather than being forced to shape fiscal and monetary policies according to demands of fickle financial markets.

How would the Tobin Tax benefit people?

By making crises less likely, the tax would help avoid the social devastation that occurs in the wake of a financial crisis. It could also be a significant source of global revenue at a time when foreign aid is decreasing and strong domestic anti-tax sentiments are reducing the ability of governments to raise revenue. In the face of increasing income disparity and social inequity, the Tobin Tax represents a rare opportunity to capture the enormous wealth of an untaxed sector and redirect it towards the public good.

Conservative estimates show the tax could yield from $150–300 billion annually. The UN estimates that the cost of wiping out the worst forms of poverty and environmental destruction globally would be around $225 billion per year.

Who will be taxed?

The majority of foreign-exchange dealing is by 100 of the world's largest banks. The top 10 control 52 per cent of the market and are mostly American, German and British. Citigroup tops the list with a 7.75-percent market share and a 1998 volume of foreign exchange transactions which, at $8.5 trillion, exceeded the GDP of the United States. These banks operate in their own interest and on behalf of large corporate and private investors, insurance companies, hedge funds, mutual funds and pension funds.

What will be taxed?

Only specialized financial transactions known as "spots," "swaps," "futures" and "forwards" will be taxed. With the exception of spot transactions, these instruments are known as derivatives because their value is derived from the value of an underlying asset which is not bought or sold in the transaction.

Tourists exchanging dollars to pay for their holidays abroad would not be subject to a Tobin Tax. Debate continues as to whether the tax should apply to any transaction less than a million dollars.

How does the Tobin Tax work?

The tax would target only speculative currency transactions. Because it is not easy to determine which types of transactions are speculative and which are associated with legitimate trade in goods and services, the tax hinges on the speed of a transaction. Speed is the primary difference between speculative and legitimate trade. Productive investment works on the medium-to-long-term while speculators flip investments like pancakes, profiting by the daily, hourly and minute-to-minute fluctuations in interest rates and currency values. Eighty per cent of all speculative transactions occur within seven days or less—40 per cent occur in two days or less.

A Tobin Tax would automatically penalize short-term exchanges, while barely affecting the incentives for commodity trading and long-term capital investments.

Won't speculators find ways to evade the tax?

Inevitably. However, this has never dissuaded governments from collecting taxes, particularly sin taxes designed to stem unacceptable behavior. The real question is, how do you minimize evasion?

A Tobin Tax could be difficult to evade. Because currency transactions are tracked electronically, in theory the tax would be easy to collect through the computer systems that record each trade. While the amount of money is enormous, the number of centers where trading occurs and the number of traders is not. Eighty per cent of foreign-exchange trading takes place in just seven cities. Agreement by London, New York and Tokyo alone would capture 58 per cent of speculative trading.

Won't speculators shift operations to offshore tax havens?

Agreement between nations could help avoid the relocation threat, particularly if the tax were charged at the site where dealers or banks are physically located or at the sites where payments are settled or "netted." The relocation of Chase Manhattan Bank to an offshore site would be expensive, risky and highly unlikely—particularly to avoid a small tax.

Globally, the move towards a centralized trading system means transactions are being tracked by fewer and fewer institutions. Hiding trades is becoming increasingly difficult. Transfers to tax havens like the Cayman Islands could be penalized at double the agreed rate or more. Citizens of participating countries would also be taxed regardless of where the transaction was carried out.

What is the biggest barrier to the Tobin Tax?

It's not technical or administrative. It's political. The tax is seen as a threat by the financial community and has met with stiff resistance by a sector with massive political clout. The very idea of putting people ahead of markets challenges the foundations of the current global economic model and those who control it.

Can the opposition be overcome?

In the wake of recent global financial crises, governments everywhere are examining their faith in free markets. Even the World Bank and the International Monetary Fund recently praised Malaysia's use of capital controls to jump-start its battered economy. This is a fundamental shift in attitude, unimaginable only a year ago.

The political appeal of this tax to cash-strapped governments and multilateral agencies worldwide can't be underestimated. And voters will likely respond well to a campaign to tax big banks, which are widely viewed as under-taxed.

Who supports the Tobin Tax?

The international trade union movement, the Canadian Parliament, the Finnish Government and a growing number of academics and elected representatives. In Brazil politicians recently launched the "Parliamentary Front for the Tobin Tax." And citizens' movements for a Tobin Tax are active around the world, including CIDSE in Europe, Attac in France, the Halifax Initiative in Canada, KEPA in Finland, War on Want in Britain, and the Tobin Tax Initiative in the United States. These and other groups have established the International Tobin Tax Network to share information and coordinate actions as they work to build public and political support for the tax.

This is only one aspect of the fundamental reform of the global financial system and is not a panacea for the world's financial ills and development woes. The democratization of economic decision-making and the equitable redistribution of wealth must become the central principles upon which governments act in the new millennium.

The victory in Canada is an important first step, but the real work has just begun. Citizens and politicians around the world must not let the powerful forces who oppose the Tobin Tax stifle, manipulate and ultimately undermine an essential public debate on controlling global financial markets.

The Tobin Tax deserves a fair hearing. Only widespread popular support and public pressure can ensure it.

The debt is used as a justification to maintain neoliberal policies, including what are known as structural adjustment programs, as institutional mechanisms to perpetuate a state of dependence. Bail-out programs by creditors, with the support of the International Monetary Fund and the World Bank have only served to ensure the continuity for mechanisms to keep countries deep in debt.

Tegucigalpa Declaration,
Latin American and Caribbean Jubilee 2000 Platform, Tegucigalpa, Honduras, January 27, 1999

23

Rewriting the Rules for Global Investment

Tony Clarke

When negotiations for a Multilateral Agreement on Investment (MAI) began to fall apart in the Spring of 1998, pundits and journalists took stock of the international citizens' campaign that had turned the tables on the architects of economic globalization.

Britain's venerable *Financial Times* (FT) referred to the final scene from the movie *Butch Cassidy and the Sundance Kid* when the two amiable but confused American crooks wind up in Latin America facing the Bolivian military. The FT used the scene to portray the bewilderment which overcame Western leaders as the MAI unraveled.

> Picture a group of politicians and diplomats looking over their shoulders at an encroaching horde of vigilantes whose motives and methods are only dimly understood in most national capitals, asking despairingly: "Who are these guys?"

Praising the effectiveness of the anti-MAI campaign, one veteran trade diplomat said: "This episode is a turning point. It means we have to rethink our approach to international economic and trade negotiations."

A rethink is certainly overdue. But it may come as a surprise to the MAI's well-heeled backers that the deal's critics were not flatly opposed to the idea of a global investment treaty. Instead, many anti-MAI campaigners insisted that a totally different kind of global treaty was needed—one that would bring transnational corporations under the rule of law rather than provide them with a bill of rights and freedoms, as the MAI did.

So how do we begin to construct an Alternative Investment Treaty that is fundamentally at odds with the current neo-liberal orthodoxy?

The first step is to review the basic goals of investment. Capital needs to be seen primarily as an instrument or means of development, not as tool for turning a quick profit at the expense of people and the earth. Specifically, investment should serve the priorities of just and sustainable development. Nor is this just pie-in-the-sky. The building blocks have already been laid in numerous covenants and charters of the United Nations.

Take the 1948 Universal Declaration of Human Rights and its accompanying Covenant on Economic, Social and Cultural Rights; or the UN Covenant on Civil and Political Rights. Together they assert the supremacy of democratic rights and freedoms over political and economic tyranny. These covenants have been reinforced by more recent charters from the Rio Summit on the Environment, the Beijing Summit on Women and the Copenhagen Summit on Social Development.

What's more, the 1974 UN Charter on the Economic Rights and Duties of States recognized the responsibilities of national governments to regulate foreign investment in order to serve the economic, social and environmental priorities of development. At the center of this Charter is the principle that capital has "social obligations." This means that capital formation is a social process built on present and previous generations of human labor. Businesses use both economic and social infrastructure, things like roads and bridges and services like public education, sanitation and clean water.

They also make use of natural resources extracted from the earth for energy and production. For these reasons there is both a social and an ecological mortgage on all capital—corporations have a debt to pay back to both society and nature. This "stored value" of capital provides legitimate grounds for putting obligations on investors.

Such a reassessment won't happen without changing both the venue and process of negotiations. As a rich-nations club where the world's most powerful companies are based, the Organization for Economic Co-operation and Development is not the place to hammer out an alternative treaty along these lines. Nor is the World Trade Organization (WTO). Although the WTO includes most of the world's nation-states, its power structure is heavily weighted against the developing countries.

The only appropriate place is the UN itself. Despite disturbing signs of corporate infiltration in UN affairs, the foundation for developing an alternative framework is located there, along with more equitable decision-making. What is required is leadership within UN circles to kick-start the process.

An Alternative Investment Treaty
Main Principles

Citizens' Rights—Investment should be designed to ensure that capital serves the basic rights and needs of all citizens including: human rights (adequate food, clothing, shelter); social rights (quality healthcare, education, social services); labor rights (employment, fair wages, unions, health and safety standards); environmental rights (protection of air, water, forests, fish, wildlife and non-renewable resources) and cultural rights (preservation of peoples' identity, values, customs, heritage).

State Responsibilities—To ensure this, governments have the right and responsibility to regulate the national economy, including the protection of: strategic areas of their economies (finance, energy, communications) by establishing public enterprises; and sensitive areas known as the "commons" (the environment, healthcare, culture) through government-run public services.

Corporate Obligations—Although foreign-based corporations can expect fair treatment and a reasonable return on investment (compensation for expropriation of assets) they must maintain certain social obligations such as performance standards designed to ensure citizens' basic needs and rights. They must also recognize that governments have the right to protect and enhance strategic areas of their economies and the "commons." And they must contribute a portion of their capital to the "commons" by paying their fair share of taxes.

Key Elements

Fair Treatment—Foreign investment would be welcome provided social obligations were met. The concept of "national treatment," which is used to force governments to treat foreign corporations on the same terms as domestic companies, should be discarded. Instead the "stored value" of capital would be the basis for establishing obligations for fair treatment of foreign-based corporations.

Social Obligations—Governments have the legal right to require all corporations, both foreign and domestic, to meet basic social obligations such as labor standards, environmental safeguards and social-security contributions.

Performance Standards—To ensure that foreign investment serves national-development priorities, governments would be allowed to require standards such as job quotas, balancing imports with exports, quotas on natural resource exports or restrictions on the repatriation of profits. In return for access to a country's markets and resources, a government could require that a foreign company create a specified number of new jobs in the community or adhere to restrictions on the export of non-renewable resources. Canada's Foreign Investment Review Act once provided the Canadian Government with the policy tools to apply this kind of performance requirement on foreign investments.

Investment Incentives—To ensure that corporations keep these social obligations, governments may use investment "incentives" including: grants, loans and subsidies; procurement practices; tax incentives and limits on profit remittances for foreign companies that fail their social obligations. Governments could decide, for example, to buy from either foreign or domestic companies as a way of attracting productive investment.

Public Enterprises—All governments have a responsibility to use tax revenues for protecting the "commons" through public investments. These could include exercising public ownership over key sectors of the economy; establishing social programs and public services; safeguarding ecologically sensitive areas; protecting cultural heritage.

Expropriation Measures—Fair compensation should be paid to foreign corporations whose physical assets are expropriated for public purposes, but not when social or environmental regulations add to business costs. Compensation should be determined by national law with due regard to the value of the initial investment, the valuation of the properties for tax purposes, and the amount of wealth taken out of the country during the period of investment. A foreign corporation could not demand compensation for an environmental law that placed a quota on the export of a non-renewable resource nor a health ban on the sale of toxic substances, on the grounds that such measures would reduce the corporation's profit margins. Nor could a foreign company claim compensation for loss of future profits because government actions prevent a planned investment from going ahead.

Financial Transactions—All governments have a right to require that foreign investment be used for productive rather than speculative purposes; that foreign corporations deposit a percentage of their profits in the central bank for a specified minimum period; that foreign-exchange transactions be taxed in order to slow down currency speculation. For example, to prevent the sudden exodus of speculative capital from Chile, "speed bump" measures were introduced which required investment to remain in the country for at least a year.

Dispute Settlement—In the event of a dispute, citizens, governments and corporations all have the right to be heard. Disputes filed by citizens would be heard by national courts which would have powers to invoke injunctions and award monetary compensation. Through this process any one of the three parties with legal standing could bring a suit for monetary compensation but not for violation of the investment rules aimed at striking down national laws. To ensure that NGOs, native communities, environment and women's groups, trade unions and others have equal access to the dispute-settlement mechanism, national and international funds should be established for citizen intervenors.

Fortunately, there is much agreement already over the substance of core labor rights. Last year, business, labor, and government representatives from 173 nations reaffirmed core labor standards as fundamental human rights, including freedom of association and the right to organize and bargain collectively. They also called for the elimination of forced labor, child labor, and employment-related discrimination. Virtually every independent labor federation has endorsed the ICFTU's [International Confederation of Free Trade Unions] call for building labor rights into the global trading system. The divide is not between North and South; it is between workers everywhere and the great concentrations of capital and the governments they dominate.

Jay Mazur, President,
UNITE (Union of Needletrades, Industrial and Textile Employees)
Chair of AFL-CIO International Affairs Committee

24

Fair Trade, Not Free Trade

Deborah James

More and more people are demanding that corporations must pay living wages in order for people to buy their products. After a few years of sweatshop exposés and increased global labor struggles, most people in the United States would rather buy a product made under fair trade conditions than under sweatshop labor conditions.

According to a recent consumer study, 78 percent of consumers would rather purchase a product associated with a cause in which they believe, and 54 percent said that they would pay more for a product that supports their cause. A 1997 consumer study by TransFairUSA revealed that 49 percent of specialty coffee drinkers surveyed said they would buy Fair Trade coffee.

We rightly resist allowing ourselves to be defined primarily as consumers in a society based on consumption. We resist the marketers and free trade advocates who try to define freedom as the freedom to consume the most or cheapest or most luxurious products. Yet to deny our *power* as consumers is to abandon an immense influence that, when *organized*, we can use for positive change.

Historically consumer organizations have existed to protect consumers from fraudulent product marketing, such as quack medicine or false nutrition claims. They have also served to demand increased car safety, organic foods, fire-resistant children's clothing, nutrition labeling, truth in advertising and much more.

Recently consumer associations have been a leading force in the debate around the safety of genetically modified organisms in our food supply. But the question remains, can we organize ourselves as consumers to demand not only safer and better quality products for ourselves, but safer, healthier and more just working conditions for the producers of the products we buy?

Fair Trade, thrust into popular consciousness during the WTO protests in Seattle, means different things to different people. As an oppositional ideology to free trade, its essence is an approach to trade policies that benefit workers, communities and the environment, rather than multinational corporations. This approach demands change of the existing multilateral structures and agreements. Another aspect seeks to propose alternative agreements such as the HOPE for Africa Bill or the Alternative Agreement for the Americas, which include provisions such as debt cancellation, labor rights and environmental protections. A third aspect of Fair Trade, however, involves bypassing the existing structures and creating our own model of global trade, based on economic justice and community development.

Fair Trade means an equitable and fair partnership between marketers in North America and producer groups in Asia, Africa, Latin America and other parts of the world. Fair Traders agree to abide by the following criteria:

- Paying a fair wage in the local context;
- Offering employees opportunities for advancement;
- Providing equal employment opportunities for all people;
- Engaging in environmentally sustainable practices;
- Being open to public accountability;
- Building long-term trade relationships;
- Providing healthy and safe working conditions within the local context;
- Providing financial and technical assistance to producers whenever possible.

In the United States, the Fair Trade Federation is the national alliance of retailers, wholesalers, producers and consumers who support living wages for artisans and farmers according to Fair

Trade criteria. Fair Traders are actively involved in educating their customers about the working conditions of the people who produce the products they sell.

The amount and quality of Fair Trade goods brought into the United States has increased dramatically over the last several years. Products include those based on primarily traditional skills such as textile weaving, pottery and silversmithing, as well as products designed specifically for environmental conservation such as paper handmade from local renewable plants.

"United to Live Better" (UPAVIM) expresses the activities of a group of women in the poverty-stricken barrio of *La Esperanza* (in Guatemala City) who organized themselves into a community organization. UPAVIM oversees the development and operation of health and education programs which benefit the people of La Esperanza, including medical and dental clinics and a laboratory, a well-baby program, a breast-feeding program directed by the La Leche League of Guatemala, a day care center, and a children's scholarship and tutoring program that sends more than 500 children to public school and provides the tutoring support to keep them there. Key to the UPAVIM programs is the production and sale of the crafts and clothing marketed through fair trade groups. Sale of these items provides direct income for the women as well as crucial financial support for the various programs.

While the percentage of total world trade that is Fair Trade is quite small, it represents both an important model as well as important income for the hundreds of thousands of producers worldwide who receive fair wages for their work.

The Fair Trade movement is many times stronger in Europe than in the United States. Over 2,500 stores are part of the Network of European World Shops. The European wholesaler alliance (the European Fair Trade Association) has member organizations from nine countries who import from 550 producer groups around the world. And the International Federation for Alternative Trade includes 143 Fair Trade organizations in 47 countries.

Setting up an alternative network of distribution may not be the answer in every sector: it may work for traditional craft products but it is not likely to be a solution for the steel industry. Yet Fair Trade does demonstrate that it is possible to operate a business and import from developing countries while empowering workers and conserving the environment.

The Coffee Alternative

There is one highly-traded commodity for which there is an international system of Fair Trade certification that is making its debut in the United States—coffee.

Coffee is the world trading system's second most valuable legal commodity (behind oil), with over 10 billion pounds exported each year from over 70 countries. With over 130 million North Americans drinking coffee, the United States consumes over one-fourth of the world supply.

About half of all coffee worldwide is produced by small farmers. These farmers own and farm their own small plots of land, but have little or no control over the export system for their coffee. "Free trade" in the coffee industry means farmers generally receive between 30 and 50 cents per pound of coffee that retails for as much as $10-$12 per pound in gourmet coffee markets. Small farmers working without the benefit of an organized export cooperative are forced to sell to exploitative middlemen who generally pay them less than half of the export price. This export price is based on the New York "C" Contract spot price and is usually around $1 per pound, but fluctuates wildly. Like most raw export commodities, when the price goes up, the exporters benefit and consumers pay more; when the price goes down, the farmers gets gouged yet consumer prices often remain high.

Fair Trade seeks to correct these imbalances by setting a minimum price per pound. This international Fair Trade price, $1.26 per pound, is set by the Fair Trade Labeling Organizations International (FLO) which includes farmer cooperatives. When market prices go above this level, farmers get the market price plus a five cent premium. But when market prices are below $1.26 per pound, as they have been for most of the last decade, the farmers still get the floor price: a living wage. Rather than operating on a charity model, where donations are made based on net profits of a company, Fair Trade changes the entire business model to include fair wages for workers as an integral part of the business arrangement. When prices are at $.85 per pound, as they were on November 30, 1999, Fair Trade can easily make the difference between keeping and losing the farm.

TransFairUSA is the national licensing agency that certifies importers and roasters here in the United States. They are the U.S. section of FLO, which includes monitors from 17 different countries. The International Fair Trade Registry certifies over 300 cooperatives in 20 different producer countries, representing over 550,000 farmers. The monitors in other countries—but not yet in the U.S.—also certify cocoa, honey, sugar, tea and bananas.

Fair Trade coffee goes beyond simply paying a fair price for hard work, as the workers actually own the means of production (especially land) and have much more control over the means of distribution (direct export). For a farmer group to get on the International Fair Trade Registry, they have to meet two basic criteria; they have to be small farmers (the Fair Trade system does not certify plantation estates) and they have to be organized. This means that they have their own system for ensuring democratic distribution of profits and providing for community development. Monitoring then, serves not as a substitute for independent labor organizing, but as a way to ensure that importers and roasters are adhering to Fair Trade criteria of paying a fair market price to worker-owned production cooperatives.

Fair Trade criteria also address the needs for credit and technical assistance. In addition, serious Fair Traders such as Equal Exchange and Thanksgiving Coffee (pioneer Fair Trade coffee companies) build long-term relationships with farmers and treat them as equals in the business partnership.

Other key issues in coffee production include organic and shade grown methods of production. These primarily address environmental concerns, but have significant advantages for small producers because farmers often receive premiums for organic and shade grown coffee. Farmers also obviously benefit by working on land free of pesticide pollution, increasing financial security through crop diversity, and being less beholden to expensive inputs of chemical fertilizers and pesticides. Most of the regions that produce organic and shade grown coffees also participate in Fair Trade cooperatives: primarily Mexico, as well as Central America and the Andean countries of South America. While 85 percent of coffee produced by Fair Trade cooperatives is organic and shade grown, a large part of the coffee grown under organic and shade conditions are not sold at Fair Trade prices.

Fair Trade cooperatives last year together produced over 60 million pounds of coffee, yet were only able to sell half of that coffee at Fair Trade terms. That means there are over 30 million pounds still available in the Fair Trade market. The big gap is U.S. consumption; U.S. importers purchase one in every four pounds in the world market but most are not buying Fair Trade. Dozens of small roasters have already signed on to be Fair Trade Certified; but there are over 1,000 coffee roasters—including the major chains such as Starbucks—that have yet to sign on. We need to demonstrate to them that there is a serious demand for Fair Trade in the coffee industry by organizing Fair Trade campaigns in every town together with campuses, churches, unions, farmers, environmental and solidarity groups.

WTO Challenges

Various efforts have been made by industry leaders in past years to limit the use of voluntary labels. Timber and paper corporations have sought to ban labels such as "sustainably harvested" and "recycled" by getting them declared WTO-illegal on the basis that they unfairly prejudice consumers towards certain products based on methods of production. World Trade Organization rules do not allow differential treatment of a product based on its method of production. But these labels are voluntary, not obligatory, and they are as important for consumer choice as product content and nutritional information.

Don't we have a right to know if a product we buy was produced in a sweatshop or with living wages? We have the right to know how a product affects our own bodies, so shouldn't we have the right to know how it affects the earth and how it affects the people who produced it? Shouldn't companies that voluntarily follow sustainability and social justice criteria be legally able to communicate that message to consumers eager to make consumer choices according to their beliefs about the importance of living wages?

Making Fair Trade a viable economic system and a widespread consumer preference through coffee is a strategically important effort. It demonstrates that there are consumers willing to shift purchasing preferences based on conditions of production. It demonstrates that workers in the U.S. stand in solidarity with workers and farmers in developing countries in demanding living wages and just economic systems. It demonstrates that environmentalists recognize the links between living wages and ecology. And it enables us to demonstrate that there is a viable way of conducting global trade based on economic justice and environmental sustainability rather than corporate profits, cheap labor and resource extraction.

> *Despite the adoption of sometimes painful economic reforms by many African countries over the past two decades, the promised benefits of trade liberalization—increased foreign direct investment, easier access to Northern markets and expanded technology transfer and technical assistance—have not materialized. Fully 70 percent of the wealth generated by trade liberalization has flowed to developed countries and, by some measures, the current rules governing world trade—set largely by the industrialized countries over the course of the 1986-94 Uruguay Round agreements—have only contributed to Africa's economic woes.*
>
> Mike Fleshman, *Africa Recovery*

25

Why and How to Pressure the World Bank

Kevin Danaher

The World Bank controls more "development" capital and has more policy influence in the developing countries than any other institution. The Bank's policies and its ideology are seriously flawed, and these flaws result in widespread human suffering and environmental destruction. If we really care about the future of the planet, we must struggle to transform the World Bank.

Below are some arguments you may find useful in educating people about the World Bank. We conclude this chapter with information on the Bankrupt the World Bank Campaign, which is working to take away the World Bank's main source of funding.

1. The World Bank promotes globalization of market forces, which creates greater inequality.

Over the past 50 years the globalization of the economy—led by the World Bank, the International Monetary Fund and transnational corporations—has proceeded at a quickening pace. These institutions have pressured governments to remove barriers to the cross-border flows of money and products.

This globalization of market forces has greatly increased inequality. The United Nations Development Programme (UNDP) reports in its 1998 *Human Development Report* that the richest

20 percent of the world's population consumes 86 percent of the world's resources, and the poorest 80 percent of the world's people account for just 14 percent of global consumption spending.

This extreme inequality results in a child dying from the effects of hunger on an average of one every four seconds. Children are dying needlessly from malnutrition-related diseases, diseases for which the vaccine costs a few cents, and gastroenteritis caused by drinking bad water (the "cure" consisting of clean water with a bit of sugar and salt). Millions of children suffer like this because in a market economy you only get things if you have the money to pay for them. Relying on market forces means consigning billions of people to a degrading life of suffering and injustice.

2. The World Bank is wrong in arguing that economic growth will solve the problems we face.

World Bank officials keep reassuring us that if we can just get economic growth rates high enough, these problems will be solved. We regularly hear the refrain, "a rising tide floats all boats." But for those who don't own boats or who have leaky boats, a rising tide means greater inequality between them and the more fortunate.

Even World Bank data shows that market-driven "growth" is making things worse, not better. Look at a period of rapid economic growth such as 1960 to the present. During that period the global economy experienced rapid growth in all the major indicators: foreign direct investment, international trade, international debt, and global GNP. Did inequality in the world get better or worse during that period? It got far worse. Did inequality *within* most countries get better or worse? It got far worse. Did environmental destruction get better or worse during that period? It got far worse.

3. The real function of the World Bank is *not* to promote "development" but rather to integrate the ruling elites of third world countries into the global system of rewards and punishments dominated by elites from the industrial countries.

Because direct colonial control of the third world is no longer tolerated, northern elites need an indirect way to control policies implemented by third world governments. By getting the elites onto a debt treadmill and promising them new cash if they implement policies written in Washington, the World Bank can effectively control third world policies.

Think of how a typical infusion of capital from the World Bank or the IMF transpires. The well-paid officials of the multilateral lending institutions meet with local elites (mainly political leaders but also business tycoons and generals) and agree to lend huge amounts of money if the local elites are willing to implement policies crafted in Washington and Wall Street. These policies call for: keeping your economy open to foreign capital; allowing liberal repatriation of profits; keeping wages, trade unions and environmental restrictions to a minimum; balancing the government's budget (often by cutting social services); and focusing economic strategy on exporting raw and semi-processed goods to the markets of the global north.

After signing on the dotted line, the local elites have great leeway in how they will spend the money. That is why the third world is plagued by overspending on the military (used more to keep unpopular elites in power than to protect against foreign enemies), and an abundance of "white elephant" projects that were overseen by some dictator's son-in-law.

So the main *function* of institutions such as the World Bank and the IMF is to maintain the transnational alliance of elites. If third world elites are more accountable to Washington and Wall Street than to their own people, there will never be real development or real democracy.

4. Evidence from many countries shows that the policies promoted by the World Bank are disastrous.

Whether you look at poor countries such as Somalia, Rwanda and Mozambique or well-endowed countries such as Ghana, Brazil and Mexico, the policies pushed by the World Bank have worsened conditions for the majority.

Brazil is a huge country with just about every natural resource you can imagine. The country is a major producer of coffee, soybeans, corn, cocoa, sugar, oranges, animal products, wood, and a wide range of manufactured goods. The country's area of natural forest is greater than that of Canada and the U.S. combined. Yet despite Brazil's abundance, millions of Brazilians go hungry on a regular basis. There are between 7 million and 10 million abandoned children, living on the streets with no adult supervision. The steady commercialization of agriculture has pushed millions of family farmers off the land into crowded urban slums. Brazil ranks as one of the most unequal societies in the world. Although the government has been collaborating with IMF and World Bank officials in making payments on the foreign debt, Brazil is more deeply in debt now than it was twenty years ago.

Mexico is well-endowed with petroleum, good farmland, an abundant labor supply, mineral resources and forests. Yet despite some years of high GNP growth rates, the standard of living of most Mexicans is worse now than it was twenty years ago. More than half the population is either unemployed or underemployed; the purchasing power of the minimum wage has fallen to less than what it was in the 1970s; family farmers are being forced off their farms by an influx of cheap U.S. corn and other crops ushered in by the free-market policies of NAFTA; environmental destruction is mounting; poverty-driven crime has soared; and the corruption of Mexican elites (more beholden to outside money than to their own people) has become legendary.

During the 1960s, 1970s, and 1980s, South Korea rejected a free market model and instead relied on a state-interventionist approach to economic development: high tariffs to protect infant industries, state-directed investment in chosen sectors, land reform, social welfare programs, and more. Despite many years of government repression, the country did extremely well economically. But in the 1990s, when South Korean leaders listened to the free market ideologues from the U.S. Treasury Department and the World Bank and opened up their capital markets and reduced control on foreign capital penetration, their economy ended up being swamped by global financial volatility.

Across Africa there are dozens of countries that have been under the tutelage of the free-market pushers for decades, and what has it gotten them? Great amounts of wealth have been extracted from the continent, external debt and interest payments have skyrocketed, real wages have declined, social services have deteriorated, the environment has been decimated, and hopelessness is spreading.

Evidence from dozens of countries under World Bank policy control shows a similar pattern: structural adjustment policies may help countries make payments on their foreign debts and may create some millionaires but the majority of the population suffers lower wages, reduced social services and less democratic access to the policy-making process.

5. The World Bank's emphasis on expanding exports has been disastrous for the environment.

As part of the standard structural adjustment package, the World Bank encourages countries to expand their exports so they will have more hard currency (especially dollars) to make payments on their foreign debts. But this leads countries to overexploit their natural resources. They cut down their forests, which contributes to the greenhouse effect. They pump chemicals onto their land to produce export crops such as coffee, cotton and tobacco, thus poisoning their land and water while neglecting food crops. They rip minerals out of the ground at a frantic pace, endangering human lives and the environment. They overfish coastal and international waters, depleting a resource of the global commons.

Central to World Bank policies is an orientation toward the market. Yet markets are only capable of valuing things in terms of money. A tree has no value standing; only when the tree is killed and turned into toothpicks, hot tubs and other marketable commodities does it generate market value. A fish swimming has no value; only when the fish is killed does it generate market value. Thus, destroying nature is an intrinsic part of the market economy.

As long as destroying nature is profitable, and as long as there are no countervailing institutions powerful enough to stop the World Bank, the IMF, the WTO and the corporations they serve—our habitat *will* be destroyed.

6. The "free market" economic model being pushed on third world governments is *not* one that was used by the industrial countries.

All the wealthy countries—the U.S.A., Japan, Germany, England, France and the recent success stories such as Taiwan and South Korea—used a state-interventionist model, with government playing a strong role directing investment, managing trade and subsidizing chosen sectors of the economy. The U.S. was in many ways the "mother country" of protectionism. Just think of all the major U.S. industries that would not exist in their present form had it not been for massive government intervention and subsidies (railroads, avionics, computers, biotechnology, and the automobile-highway-suburbia complex). Would we have a big electronics industry or nuclear power industry were it not for that massive government subsidy called the Pentagon? What if all the government financing that was poured into nuclear power had been invested in solar power instead?

It gives hypocrisy a bad name for the U.S. government to go around the world pushing a free market model on third world countries when the historical record shows that neither we, nor any other wealthy country, used that model.

7. Globalization-from-above is being rejected and millions of people all over the world are struggling to build globalization-from-below.

Globalization-from-above is controlled by wealthy elites and driven by a hunger for more wealth and power. But there is another form of globalization made up of grassroots alliances of human rights activists, trade unions, women's organizations, environmental coalitions and farmers' organizations. This is the people's alliance that rocked the WTO in Seattle in late 1999.

This bottom-up form of globalization does not have the amount of money or guns possessed by the elites but it does have moral authority because it gives priority to meeting basic human needs and saving the environment rather than accumulating more money for the already wealthy.

This alternative vision calls for more openness and accountability by institutions such as the World Bank and transnational corporations. It calls for raising wages and health and safety standards in the third world, rather than driving first world standards downward. It calls for stewardship of natural resources to preserve the environment for our great-grandchildren to enjoy. It seeks to redefine self-interest so that it is more in line with the common interest of humanity. Yet time is running out.

How to Take Away the World Bank's Money

The World Bank gets most of its capital by selling bonds to wealthy investors. If we can pressure institutional funds (e.g., university endowments, churches, trade unions and state worker pension funds) to refrain from buying World Bank bonds, we can exert serious pressure on the Bank.

Just think about the huge impact the divestment movement had on South Africa's white minority rulers by cutting them off from their main supply of capital. The divestment struggle also raised a key question: who controls how capital is invested and why isn't it a more democratic process?

The investment portfolios of many institutions contain World Bank bonds or mutual funds that purchase World Bank bonds. The name appearing on the bonds will be the World Bank's formal name: International Bank for Reconstruction and Development (IBRD). The bonds pay relatively high rates of interest and are considered safe because they carry a AAA rating.

Once you have picked an institution, you can present your critique of why they should not own IBRD bonds. For useful information on the Bank call the 50 Years Is Enough Network (202-IMF-BANK) or check their website (www.50years.org).

For specific material on how to wage a World Bank bond boycott in your area—including a sample resolution and quotes from socially responsible investment firms concerning why they do not buy World Bank bonds—contact the Bankrupt the World

Bank Campaign (505)341-1864, www.preamble.org/cej

There is no need to research whether the institution owns any IBRD bonds; you are merely asking them to promise not to buy the bonds *in the future*. Press the authorities for a policy statement, on letterhead, saying that they will not purchase World Bank bonds.

If they blow you off, you can escalate to a more public campaign. Mobilize colleagues to gather signatures and other forms of public support for the simple demand that the institution not buy World Bank bonds. There are literally thousands of safe bonds in the marketplace, so there is no reason why any institution *needs* to buy World Bank bonds.

When you finally get them to issue the policy statement, that piece of paper will be useful to the rest of us in getting more and more institutions to enact similar policies. The *financial* impact of any one institution swearing off World Bank bonds will be small, but the public relations impact of many churches, unions and city governments announcing they will boycott World Bank bonds will strike a blow at the heart of this undemocratic institution.

Labor is prior to, and independent of, capital. Capital is only the fruit of labor, and could never have existed if labor had not first existed. Labor is the superior of capital, and deserves much the higher consideration.

President Abraham Lincoln
December 3, 1861

26

Conclusion
Ten Ways to Democratize
the Global Economy

Deborah James

*C*itizens can and should play an active role in shaping the future of our global economy. Here are some of the ways in which we can work together to reform global trade rules, demand that corporations are accountable to people's needs, build strong and free labor, and promote fair and environmentally sustainable alternatives.

1. No Globalization Without Representation

Multilateral institutions such as the World Trade Organization, the World Bank, and the International Monetary Fund create global policy with input mainly from government elites and multinational corporations, with very little input from grassroots citizens groups. We need to ensure that all global citizens must be democratically represented in the formulation, implementation, and evaluation of all global social and economic policies of the WTO, the IMF and the World Bank. The WTO must immediately halt all meetings and negotiations in order for a full, fair, and public assessment to be conducted examining the impacts of the WTO's policies to date. The WTO must be replaced by a body that is fully democratic, transparent, and accountable to citizens of the entire world instead of to corporations. We must build support for trade policies that protect workers, human rights and the environment.

Focus on the Global South www.focusweb.org
Public Citizen's Global Trade Watch/Citizens Trade Campaign
www.tradewatch.org
Third World Network www.twnside.org.sg
International Forum on Globalization www.ifg.org

2. Mandate Corporate Responsibility

Corporations have so heavily influenced global trade negotiations that they now have rights and representation greater than individual citizens and even governments. Under the guise of "free trade" they advocate weakening of labor and environmental laws—a global economy of sweatshops and environmental devastation.

Corporations must be subject to the people's will; they should have to prove their worth to society or be dismantled. Corporations must be accountable to public needs, be open to public scrutiny, provide living-wage jobs, and abide by all environmental and labor regulations. Shareholder activism is an excellent tool for challenging corporate behavior.

Program on Corporations, Law and Democracy
www.poclad.org
Campaign for Labor Rights
 www.summersault.com/~agj/clr/
Transnational Research and Action Center
www.corpwatch.org
Interfaith Center for Corporate Responsibility
www.iccr.org
United Students Against Sweatshops
 www.asm.wisc.edu/usas
Student Alliance to Reform Corporations
www.corpreform.org

3. Restructure the Global Financial Architecture

Currency speculation and the derivatives market move over $1.5 trillion daily (compared to world trade of $6 trillion annually), earning short-term profits for wealthy investors at the expense of long-term development. Many countries are beginning to implement "capital controls" in order to regulate the influence of foreign capital, and grassroots groups are advocating the restructuring and regulation of the global financial architecture. Citizens can pass local city resolutions for the Tobin Tax: a tax of 0.1 percent to 0.25 percent on currency transactions which would (1) provide a disincentive for speculation but not affect real capital investment, and (2) create a huge fund for building schools & clinics throughout the world.

Tobin Tax Initiative   www.ceedweb.org/noframe.htm

Friends of the Earth   www.foe.org

Institute for Policy Studies   www.ips-dc.org

4. Cancel all Debt, End Structural Adjustment and Defend Economic Sovereignty

Debt is crushing most poor countries' ability to develop as they spend huge amounts of their resources servicing odious debt rather than serving the needs of their populations. Structural adjustment is the tool promoted by the IMF and World Bank to keep countries on schedule with debt payments, with programs promoting export-led development at the expense of social needs. There is an international movement demanding that all debt be cancelled in order for countries to prioritize health care, education, and real development. Countries must have the autonomy to pursue their own economic plans, including prioritizing social needs over the needs of transnational corporations.

Jubilee 2000 www.j2000usa.org

50 Years is Enough www.50years.org

End the Blockade Against Cuba www.igc.apc.org/cubasoli/cubalink.html

5. Prioritize Human Rights—Including Economic Rights— in Trade Agreements

The United Nations—not the WTO—must be the strongest multilateral body. The U.S. Congress must ratify all international conventions on social and political rights. Trade rules must comply with higher laws on human rights as well as economic and labor rights included in the Universal Declaration of Human Rights. We should promote alternative trade agreements that include fair trade, debt cancellation, micro-credit, and local control over development policies.

Global Exchange Corporate Accountability Campaign
www.globalexchange.org/economy/corporations
International Labor Rights Fund www.laborrights.org
HOPE for Africa Act www.citizen.org/pctrade/Africa/
HOPE/hopehome.htm
Alternative Agreement for the Americas
www.globalexchange.org/economy/alternatives/americas/

6. Promote Sustainable Development—Not Consumption— as the Key to Progress

Global trade and investment should not be ends in themselves, but rather the instruments for achieving equitable and sustainable development, including protection for workers and the environment. Global trade agreements should not undermine the ability of each nation, state or local community to meet its citizens' social, environmental, cultural or economic needs. International development should not be export-driven, but rather should prioritize food security, sustainability, and democratic participation.

Redefining Progress www.rprogress.org
Food First www.foodfirst.org
Institute for Agriculture and Trade Policy www.iatp.org

7. Integrate Women's Needs in All Economic Restructuring

Women make up half the world but hold less than five percent of positions of power in determining global economic policy, and own an estimated one percent of global property. Family survival around the world depends on the economic independence of women. Economic policies need to take into account women's important role in nutrition, education, and development. This includes access to family planning as well as education, credit, job training, policy decision-making, and other needs.

> *Women's EDGE: Economic Development and Global Equality* www.womensedge.org
>
> *International Center for Research on Women* www.icrw.org
>
> *Women's Environment and Development Organization* www.wedo.org

8. Build Free and Strong Labor Unions Internationally and Domestically

As trade becomes more deregulated, labor unions are still restricted from organizing in many countries. The International Labor Organization should have enforcement power as strong as the WTO. The U.S. government should ratify ILO conventions and set an example in terms of enforcing workers' rights to organize and bargain collectively. As corporations increase their multinational strength, unions are working to build bridges across borders and organize globally. Activists can support their efforts and ensure that free labor is an essential component of any trade agreements.

> *American Federation of Labor/Congress of Industrial Organizations* www.aflcio.org/home.htm
>
> *International Confederation of Free Trade Unions* www.icftu.org
>
> *International Labor Organization* www.ilo.org
>
> *Open World Conference* www.geocities.com/owc_2000

9. Develop Community Control Over Capital; Promote Socially Responsible Investment

Local communities should not be beholden to the IMF, the World Bank or transnational corporations. Communities should be able to develop investment and development programs that suit local needs including passing anti-sweatshop purchasing restrictions, promoting local credit unions and local barter currency, and implementing investment policies for their local governments, churches, and unions that reflect social responsibility criteria.

ACORN www.acorn.org

Sustainable America www.sanetwork.org

United for a Fair Economy www.stw.org

Alliance for Democracy www.afd-online.org

10. Promote Fair Trade, Not Free Trade

While we work to reform "free trade" institutions and keep corporate chain stores out of our neighborhoods, we should also promote our own vision of Fair Trade. We need to build networks of support and education for grassroots trade and trade in environmentally sustainable goods. We can promote labeling of goods such as Fair Trade Certified, organic, and sustainably harvested. We can purchase locally made goods and locally grown foods that support local economies and cooperative forms of production and trade.

Fair Trade Federation www.fairtradefederation.com

Rural Coalition www.farmworkers.org/rcpage.html

TransFairUSA www.transfairusa.org

Co-op America www.coopamerica.org

Global Exchange www.globalexchange.org

A special group that deserves mention because of the important role they have played training activists for mass nonviolent protests, such as the one in Seattle, is the Ruckus Society, 2054 University Ave., Suite 204, Berkeley, CA 94704 (510)848-9565. Check their websites: www.ruckus.org and www.globalizethis.org

Contributors

Seth Ackerman is a Media Analyst with *Extra!*, the magazine of FAIR, the Media Watch Group based in New York.

David Bacon is a writer, photographer and radio host living in Berkeley, CA.

Juliette Beck works in Global Exchange's Global Democracy Program.

Walden Bello is the Director of Focus on the Global South in Bangkok, Thailand. His most recent book is *A Siamese Tragedy: Development and Disintegration in Modern Thailand.*

Medea Benjamin is an author of many books, a co-founder of Global Exchange, and is the Director of Global Exchange's Global Democracy Program.

Roger Burbach is the Director of CENSA, the Center for the Study of the Americas in Berkeley, CA. His most recent book is *Globalization and Its Discontents: The Rise of Postmodern Socialisms.*

Ken Butigan is an adjunct professor at the Franciscan School of Theology and the Graduate Theological Union in Berkeley, California.

Tony Clarke is Director of the Polaris Institute in Ottawa, Canada. He is the co-author (with Maude Barlow) of three books on the MAI (Multilateral Agreement on Investments).

Kevin Danaher is a co-founder of Global Exchange and editor of *Corporations Are Gonna Get Your Mama: Globalization and the Downsizing of the American Dream*, and *50 Years Is Enough: The Case Against the World Bank and the International Monetary Fund*.

Susan George is a noted author and member of the Transnational Institute in Amsterdam. Her most recent book is *The Lugano Report*.

William Greider is National Affairs Correspondent for *The Nation*. He is the author of *One World, Ready Or Not: The Manic Logic of Global Capitalism*.

Paul Hawken is the author of many books, the newest of which is *Natural Capitalism*. He is the director of the Natural Capital Institute in Sausalito, CA.

Luis Hernandez Navarro is an editor and columnist at the Mexcio City daily *La Jornada*.

Deborah James is the Director of Global Exchange's Fair Trade Coffee Program.

Martin Khor is a prominent author and is the director of the Third World Network based in Penang, Malaysia.

Manning Marable is the Director of the Institute for Research in African-American Studies at Columbia University in New York.

Elizabeth (Betita) Martinez is a longtime activist and teacher who has written six books on social movements in the Americas. She founded the Institute for MultiRacial Justice in San Francisco.

Peter Rosset is the Executive Director of the Institute for Food and Development Policy.

Robin Round is with the Halifax Initiative, a coalition of Canadian NGOs working for the democratization of economic decision-making.

Vandana Shiva is an internationally renowned writer and activist. Her most recent book is *Stolen Harvest: The Hijacking of the Global Food Supply*.

Steven Shrybman is Executive Director of the West Coast Environmental Law Association. He is author of *The Citizen's Guide to the World Trade Organization*.

Starhawk is an author, nonviolence trainer and practitioner of the arts of magical activism. She has written many books, the most recent of which is *Walking to Mercury*.

Index

GLOBAL EXCHANGE

Global Exchange has what you need to get involved. Here are some of our programs.

- **Reality Tours**: We provide participants with a *feel* for the people of a country. We meet with farmers, human rights and peace activists, church workers, environmentalists, government officials and opposition leaders. We visit Cuba, Mexico, Haiti, South Africa, Ireland, Brazil, Vietnam and other fascinating locations. We also feature California tours investigating issues such as immigration, chemical vs. organic agriculture, and the struggle over the ancient redwoods.

- **Public Education**: Global Exchange publishes books and pamphlets on a wide range of issues: world hunger, free trade vs. fair trade, the IMF & World Bank, Mexico, Cuba, Brazil and many other issues. We also make regular radio appearances, and organize conferences and workshops. Our Speakers Bureau provides colleges and community groups with inspiring speakers on subjects such as elite globalization vs. people's globalization, how to work in the Third World, the World Trade Organization, and U.S. foreign policy.

- **Fair Trade**: To help build economic justice from the ground up, Global Exchange promotes Fair Trade that benefits low-income producers and artisan co-ops. Sales at our Berkeley and San Francisco fair trade stores and from our website support thousands of craftspeople in more than 30 developing countries and help educate people here about foreign cultures and international trade.

- **Human Rights Work**: By putting outside eyes and ears into conflict situations, Global Exchange helps report on and restrain repressive government forces. We arrange election observation teams, produce human rights reports and bring long-term volunteers into conflict zones such as the southern Mexican state of Chiapas.

- **Material Assistance**: Global Exchange provides money and technical support to successful grassroots groups in Mexico, Cuba, Vietnam, Cambodia, South Africa, the United States and other countries. Our assistance has ranged from supporting a peasant-run literacy program in Honduras to providing scholarships for poor rural girls in Vietnam to continue their educations.

See the next page for how you can get involved in Global Exchange's programs.

Global Exchange works to create more justice and economic opportunity in the world. The heart of our work is the involvement of thousands of supporters around the country.

When you become a member of Global Exchange you get:

- our quarterly newsletter and Action Alerts;
- priority on our Reality Tours to dozens of foreign countries and domestic destinations;
- a 10 percent discount on our educational materials and the crafts we sell at our third world craft stores;
- regular updates on our material aid campaigns and our support for development projects.

Plus, you get connected to a growing international network of concerned citizens working to transform the world from the bottom up.

Please use the coupon below to join Global Exchange today.

YES, I support Global Exchange's efforts to reform the global economy. Here is my tax-deductible membership donation:

___ $100   ___ $50   ___ $35   ___ $25

Name_____

Address_____

City_____State_____Zip____

Phone_____ Email_____

GLOBAL EXCHANGE

2017 Mission Street, Suite 303, San Francisco, CA 94110
(415) 255-7296, FAX (415) 255-7498
email: info@globalexchange.org
website: www.globalexchange.org